DATE DUE

BRODART   Cat. No. 23-221

Strategic environmental assessment

Strategic environmental assessment

Riki Therivel
Elizabeth Wilson
Stewart Thompson
Donna Heaney
David Pritchard

Earthscan Publications Ltd, London

First published in 1992 by
Earthscan Publications Limited
120 Pentonville Road, London N1 9JN

Reprinted 1994, 1995, 1999

A catalogue record for this book is available from the British Library

ISBN 1-85383-147-6

Typeset by Books Unlimited, Nottm.
Printed and bound in Great Britain by
Biddles Ltd, Guildford and King's Lynn

Earthscan Publications Limited is an editorially independent subsidiary of
Kogan Page Limited and publishes in association with the International Institute
for Environment and Development and the Word Wide Fund for Nature (UK).

Table of Contents

Preface

Contrary to prevalent opinion, 'environmental impact assessment' of human activities is not a 'green' fad of the late 1980s. In some form or other, for generations it has been an inescapable element in decision-making about the use of land. What is newer is the emergence of an entire science of techniques, and a forest of laws and policies aimed at a formal, consistent and enforceable assessment of environmental impacts. The Royal Society for the Protection of Birds (RSPB), in defending important nature conservation sites against threat, is a formal participant in several hundred planning cases each year throughout the United Kingdom. Many of these now feature environmental impact assessment (EIA) as required by European Community Directive 85/337. The RSPB has thus built up considerable experience of the laws, policy and science of EIA in practice. One theme emerging from this, and echoed in published reviews, is the inability of the current piecemeal 'project'-based EIA system to address cumulative, indirect and synergistic effects of projects, and the policy frameworks within which they are promoted: in short, it lacks a 'strategic' view.

Steps towards rectifying this are tentatively being taken. The European Commission has suggested a possible directive on EIA of 'policies, plans and programmes', and a number of researchers and land-use sectors are endeavouring to grapple with the concepts. There are lessons to be learned from partial systems already existing outside the UK. The RSPB decided to review this important subject with Oxford Polytechnic. The results are presented in this book, representing the most comprehensive and up-to-date treatment yet published: essential reading for all those involved with EIA, especially at the policy/legislative level.

The timing is significant. Discussions on the proposed EC directive will focus the debate in Europe for some time to come. This book is published as the UK completes its term as President of the European Council, and as the Community embarks on its Fifth Action Programme on the Environment in the light of the 1992 United Nations Commission on Environment and Development (UNCED) in Rio de Janeiro. On the domestic scene, the government is now reporting annually its national overview of environmental matters in the context of the UNCED framework; and the planning profession enjoys renewed morale after years of 'deregulation' and the threatened abolition of structure plans.

The RSPB is not simply in the business of fending off development likely to damage the national wildlife heritage. As this and our other publications show, we offer a positive package of policy proposals aimed at catering for the legitimate needs of local communities, industry and others, while also meeting urgent nature conservation objectives. Constructive input at the strategic policy and planning level can *prevent* the conflict that otherwise often arises. This is part of what we all stand to gain from the application of the principles of EIA at higher levels of decision-making. The ultimate prize, however, is that elusive grail of 'sustainability'. Ways of achieving it through strategic environmental assessment are discussed in the chapters that follow: it is our hope that this pioneering contribution may stimulate others in this crucial area of the environmental agenda for the 1990s.

David E. Pritchard, RSPB

Acknowledgements

We are very grateful for the generous assistance which the following people and organizations gave us, without which this book would not have been possible:

Hugh Barton, Ron Bass, Martin Baxter, Kevin Bayes, Carol Borgstrom, Brenda Boardman, Chris Braun, Barnaby Briggs, Jo Burgon, Chris Corrigan, Graham Culley, John Dowie, Mark Ellis, John Foster, Carol Hatton, Jenny Heap, Mike Hawkins, Stuart Housden, D.E. Ketcham, Richard Keymer, Rob Lake, Lucy Low Swarz, Graeme McVittie, Sue Marlow, Sandy Muirhead, Gail Murray, Ms. Rathelbont, Laurence Rose, Phil Rothwell, Sylvia Sullivan, John Taylor, Drew Thomas, David Thirling, Jo Treweek, Stephanie Tyler, Ronald van der Lee, Dieter Wagner, John Waldon, Gwyn Williams, Silvia Wilson, Robin Wynde, various county wildlife trusts and the many local planning authorities that offered both time and photocopies.

We are also grateful for permissions given to use material from the following sources in Chapter 3 and Appendix C:

Baseline Environmental Consulting's draft environmental impact report on the San Joaquin County Comprehensive Planning Program; Broad Oak Water's studies on water provision in Kent; several environmental impact statements prepared by the US Department of Energy; and the World Bank's Technical Paper No. 139.

We thank the RSPB staff at the Lodge, and especially Ahmad Ebrahimi, for their guidance and advice. Helpful information was provided by a number of regional and country RSPB offices. We are particularly grateful to Professor John Glasson from Oxford Polytechnic for his insightful comments.

Finally, we would like to thank Tim O'Hara and Nick Wilson for their patience and support.

Abbreviations

ACE	Association for the Conservation of Energy
AONB	Area of Outstanding Natural Beauty
BATNEEC	Best Available Technique(s) Not Entailing Excessive Cost
BEEP	Bristol Energy and Environment Plan
BP	British Petroleum
BPEO	Best Practicable Environmental Option
CAP	Common Agricultural Policy
CCC	Coalfield Communities Campaign
CCW	Countryside Council for Wales
CC	County Council
CCGT	Combined Cycle Gas Turbine
CEC	(a) Crown Estates Commission
	(b) Council of the European Communities
CEQA	California Environmental Quality Act
CHP	Combined Heat and Power
CPP	Comprehensive Planning Programme
CPRE	Council for the Protection of Rural England
DC	District Council
DoE	Department of the Environment
DEIR	Draft Environmental Impact Report
DGXI	EC Directorate General for Environment, Nuclear Safety and Civil Protection
DTI	Department of Trade and Industry
DTp	Department of Transport
EA	Environmental Assessment
EBRD	European Bank for Reconstruction and Development
EC	European Community
EE	Environmental Evaluation
EEA	European Environmental Agency
EEC	European Economic Community
EEO	Energy Efficiency Office
EIA	Environmental Impact Assessment
EIR	Environmental Impact Report
EIS	Environmental Impact Statement
EN	English Nature
EPA	Environmental Protection Act
ES	Environmental Statement
ESD	Ecologically Sustainable Development
ETSU	Energy Technology Support Unit
FEPA	Federal Environmental Protection Agency (Nigeria)

FMWH	Federal Ministry of Works and Housing (Nigeria)
GDP	Gross Domestic Product
GIS	Geographical Information System
GNP	Gross National Product
Govt.	government
ha	hectare
HMIP	Her Majesty's Inspectorate of Pollution
HMSO	Her Majesty's Stationery Office
HUD	US Department of Housing and Urban Development
IEA	a) Institute of Environmental Assessment
	b) International Energy Agency
IPC	Integrated Pollution Control
IPCC	Intergovernmental Panel on Climate Change
km	kilometre
MAFF	Ministry of Agriculture, Fisheries and Food
MNR	Marine Nature Reserve
MW	megawatts
n/a	not applicable
NCC	Nature Conservancy Council
NEPA	National Environmental Policy Act (US)
NEPP	National Environmental Policy Plan (Neth.)
NFFO	Non-Fossil Fuel Obligation
NGO	Non-Government Organisation
NNR	National Nature Reserve
NOI	Notice of Intent
NRA	National Rivers Authority
OECD	Organization for Economic Co-operation and Development
OFFER	Office of Electricity Regulation
OFGAS	Office of Gas Supply
PDO	Potentially Damaging Operation
PEIR	Programmatic Environmental Impact Report
PPG	Planning Policy Guidance Note
PPP	Policies, Plans and/or Programmes
PWR	Pressurised Water Reactor
RCEP	Royal Commission on Environmental Pollution
REC	Regional Electricity Company
RPG	Regional Planning Guidance
RSPB	Royal Society for the Protection of Birds
SAC	Special Area of Conservation
SACTRA	Standing Advisory Committee on Trunk Road Assessment
SCC	Surrey County Council
SEA	Strategic Environmental Assessment
SEEDS	South East Economic Development Strategy
SMOW	State Ministry of Works (Nigeria)
SNH	Scottish Natural Heritage

SoS	Secretary of State
SPA	Special Protection Area
SSSI	Site of Special Scientific Interest
SWCL	Scottish Wildlife and Countryside Link
TCPA	Town and Country Planning Association
UDP	Unitary Development Plan
UK	United Kingdom
UNCED	United Nations Conference on Environment and Development
US DOE	United States Department of Energy
UNECE	United Nations Economic Commission for Europe
UNEP	United Nations Environment Programme
UNESCO	United Nations Educational, Scientific and Cultural Organisation
USAID	United States Agency for International Development
US	United States
USCEQ	United States Council on Environmental Quality
UVP	Umweltverträglichkeitsprüfung (EIA in German)
WCED	World Commission on Environment and Development

1:

The changing context of environmental impact assessment

1.1 Introduction

Environmental impact assessment[1] (EIA) is the process of predicting and evaluating an action's impacts on the environment, the conclusions to be used as a tool in decision-making. It aims to prevent environmental degradation by giving decision-makers better information about the consequences that development actions could have on the environment, but can not, of itself, achieve that prevention. Briefly, EIA involves reviewing the existing state of the environment and the characteristics of the proposed action (and possibly alternative actions); predicting the state of the future environment with and without the action (the difference between the two is the action's impact); considering methods for reducing or eliminating any negative impacts; preparing an environmental impact statement (EIS) that discusses these points; and, after a decision is made about whether the action should proceed, possibly monitoring the actual impacts of the action. EIA, as an approach to environmental issues, can be characterized as multidisciplinary and predictive. In its most usual manifestation it is closely linked with the planning system.

Early discussions on EIA suggested that it should be applied to the earlier, more strategic, tiers of decision-making - policies, plans, and programmes (referred to generically throughout this book as PPPs) - as well as to individual projects (Montgomery, 1990; Wood, 1988). To date, EIA has primarily been carried out for projects - eg. power stations, industrial installations, housing developments.

Currently, however, the consideration of the environmental impacts of PPPs - commonly known as strategic environmental assessment (SEA) - is once again receiving increased interest. The Netherlands government set up a statutory SEA system in 1987 and is currently strengthening it. The New Zealand authorities have required the preparation of SEAs since late 1991. The European Community's (EC) Directorate General XI produced a proposed directive on SEA in early 1991, and the UK's Department of the Environment has recently recommended procedures resembling those of SEA.

In some instances, SEA is being seen solely as an extension of EIA for projects at an earlier stage in the decision-making process. However, in other instances it is seen as being closely linked to the concept of sustainability; SEA may be the most direct way of making judgements about sustainability operational.

This book discusses the development and current status of SEA worldwide, including its links with sustainability. It provides both a snapshot of the early stages of an exciting new form of policy, and a view of its future possibilities. The book focuses on the UK and EC, but many of its principles apply elsewhere as well. It should help to provide an impetus towards the establishment of powerful, effective SEA systems with close links to sustainability, rather than token 'green' policies that have little effect.

The first chapter considers systems of EIA for projects. It reviews some of the factors that limit the effectiveness of EIA in ensuring that development is not environmentally harmful, focusing particularly on EC Directive 85/337 on EIA (CEC, 1985; sections of this are given in Appendix A) and its implementation in the UK. It considers the need for EIA at higher tiers of decision-making, and the possibilities that this would have for making judgements about sustainability operational through SEA. Finally, it summarizes some current trends in the approach to environmental issues and the role of strategic environmental assessment in this.

Chapter 2 introduces principles and issues in SEA. It explains the distinctions and links between policies, plans, programmes and individual projects. SEA is discussed as a form of policy appraisal, and its potential strengths and weaknesses are explored. The chapter raises procedural issues regarding SEA, which are further addressed in subsequent chapters.

Chapter 3 reviews existing systems of SEA, particularly those of California and the Netherlands. It critically discusses the proposed EC directive on SEA and the UK government's recent activities concerning the appraisal of policies and plans. This chapter shows that SEA is feasible, but also points to a number of limitations to the effectiveness of the systems that are currently being tried. Appendix B expands on the good and bad points of some of the systems discussed in this chapter.

Chapters 4, 5 and 6 further explore the need for EIA at a more strategic level, using three case studies from the UK. Chapter 4 concerns coastlines; although these are covered in many places by protective designations, existing controls are not adequately preventing environmentally harmful development, or giving decision-making systems the right information with which to do so. Chapter 5 examines the energy sector. The lack of a national plan for energy is a major limitation to the comprehensive consideration of the impacts of energy-related activities. Chapter 6 addresses lowland heath, a rare and vulnerable habitat on which development is currently controlled by a variety of designations and through local authority development plans; again, these designations do not adequately prevent environmentally harmful development. Suggestions are made for the implementation of SEA.

Chapter 7 proposes that SEA in the future could take on a much greater role than simply expanding EIA to more strategic levels. It suggests that SEA could provide a framework for implementing the objective of sustainability, and proposes steps towards achieving this.

Appendix C discusses possible forms of methodology for SEA. It considers the best of the methodologies used in existing SEA systems, and offers thoughts on further application of SEA principles to practical situations.

1.2 The current state of environmental impact assessment

Worldwide spread of EIA

The development of EIA began more than 20 years ago in the United States with the US National Environmental Policy Act (NEPA) of 1969 (US Govt., 1970). After that, EIA regulations were rapidly established in countries such as Canada (1973), Australia (1974), West Germany (1975) and France (1976), and later worldwide. In 1985, EC Directive 85/337 made EIA mandatory in certain circumstances, and more uniform throughout the European Community than previously. EIA is now used in some form or other in most countries of the world.

The emphasis and effectiveness of these systems varies considerably. Many countries have official EIA systems established through regulations; others have non-mandatory EIA guidelines; and in others EIAs are prepared on an ad hoc basis for specific large-scale development projects. In some countries, EIA is performed only by government departments for public sector projects; in others it is performed only by private developers; and in others both the public and private sectors conduct EIAs. EIA has greatly facilitated public participation in the planning process for major projects in many countries, but only minimally if at all in others.

At present, some of the strongest EIA regulations exist in North America and Australia. In Europe, most countries have EIA systems; the EC saw a consistent system of EIA as a way, in the context of environmental policy, of preventing distortions of competition in the common market. EIA regulations and guidelines exist in many countries of South America and Asia, but their effectiveness is often limited by the need to foster economic growth even at the expense of the environment. Africa generally lags behind the other continents in its implementation of EIA: coping with the needs of its rapidly growing population, frequent and often violent changes of government, environmental calamities, and (in places) endemic corruption leaves few resources for preventive environmental management in a continent that nevertheless may need it more than any other (Harrison, 1987). Most of the EIAs in Africa and South America are carried out by development organizations such as the World Bank and USAID (Wathern, 1988).

The divide between more developed countries and less developed countries thus exists in EIA as in other forms of environmental policy. The wealthy industrialized countries are carrying out increasingly detailed EIAs for projects and considering its extension to more strategic levels of decision-making. The poorer nations carry out EIAs when required to do so to get funding, but even then the process is dogged by institutional and financial problems.

Further information on the development and current state of the EIA systems can be found, for instance in Anderson et al. (1984), Bear (1990), and Orloff (1980) for the US; Clark and Herington (1988) and Tomlinson (1986) for the UK; CEC (1991b), EIA Review, Lee and Wood (1984), Roberts and Roberts (1984), Wandesforde-Smith (1980), Wathern (1988) and Wood (1981) for the EC; and Cabrera (1984), Enyedi et al. (1987), O'Riordan and Sewell (1981) and Westman (1985) for other countries.

Constraints on the effectiveness of project EIA

The effectiveness of project EIA is hampered by a number of factors. Many of these are institutional, but technical factors such as the lack of environmental data and the underdevelopment of predictive capabilities also play a part.

The *types of projects* that tend to be subject to an imposed requirement for EIA are often limited. Projects that are frequently exempted include defence and security-related projects; agricultural and afforestation projects that may be seen as ways of preserving the viability of rural communities or of actually protecting the environment; small-scale projects such as windfarms and golf courses that of themselves may not have a significant environmental impact but that may cumulatively; and projects that are under the remit of uncooperative government agencies or of particularly powerful lobby groups. For instance in Japan a weaker form of EIA is required for power stations than for other forms of development because the powerful Ministry of International Trade and Industry argues that energy production is a matter of national importance and thus should not be impeded (Barrett and Therivel, 1991). EIA was made discretionary for many types of projects in the EC for what appear to be similar reasons.

The *information required in an EIA* is also often limited. The regulations or guidelines may not require the full range of potential impacts to be addressed: for instance, the UK's EIA system does not require the assessment of noise, ecological impacts, energy consumption or radioactive emissions. Some systems do not require the assessment of a full range of mitigation measures, or of alternative proposals. The latter omission is particularly detrimental; as the US Council on Environmental Quality noted over ten years ago, the consideration of alternatives 'is the heart of the environmental impact statement' (USCEQ, 1978).

The objectivity and thoroughness of an EIA is also influenced by the *organization that carries out the assessment*. In most countries EIAs are prepared by the project proponent, not by the local authority or a neutral government agency. Unless the project proponents feel that they can facilitate the planning approval process by preparing a particularly thorough EIS, they will normally gain little by going beyond the minimum statutory requirements. EIAs in the UK have been shown to cost between 0.000025 and 5 per cent of project costs (Coles et al., 1992); a thorough EIS is a large document and can be very expensive, while a minimal one could be considerably cheaper. The developer also could not be expected to prepare an EIS suggesting that a project's environmental impacts are so great that the project should not go ahead.

The level of *public participation* in the EIA process can also influence its effectiveness. Determining the views of local residents, and taking account of these views in the development proposal, is likely to improve the effectiveness of the subsequent EIA, but again can be an expensive and lengthy process. Many developers are concerned about making information that is potentially commercially confidential available for public scrutiny, although there is a general trend towards increasing citizen access to environmental information. Collections of environmental impact statements have been set up in many countries, both to improve public participation and as a way of improving the quality of future EIAs (Therivel, 1991).

The *decision* as to whether or not a project should go ahead is not tied solely to the results of the EIA, since a wide range of socio-political and economic factors must also be taken into account. This can lead to the EIA findings being virtually ignored or overridden by 'the national interest' or other factors. In some (mostly developing) countries, it is quite possible that the corruption of local officials overrides any attempt to improve decision-making through the use of EIA, though it must be said that very little literature exists on this subject.

Finally, techniques and procedures for *monitoring and auditing of actual environmental impacts* are still in their infancy. The predictions made in EIAs are rarely tested against what actually happens when the project is built and operated (Bisset and Tomlinson, 1988; Coles et al., 1992), so impact prediction techniques have had little chance of being improved. The concept of monitoring is universally applauded, but the costs are high and developers have understandably balked at any moves to make monitoring a legal requirement. California has one of the few EIA systems that do require monitoring, but it is also one of the wealthiest states in one of the wealthiest nations in the world.

That said, much good EIA practice has evolved in the private sector without being statutorily required, because a thorough assessment of all possible environmental problems, or public contentiousness and pollution liabilities is seen to be desirable for simple commercial operating reasons, quite apart from any others. It is therefore not correct to view EIA as a 'luxury' that those with more funds can afford.

Constraints on the effectiveness of project EIA in the EC and UK

The EC and UK provide more specific examples of limitations of project EIA. EC Directive 85/337 on the assessment of the effects of certain private and public projects (CEC, 1985) was adopted in 1985, after ten years of discussion and research, and was implemented by most of the individual member states three years later. The directive requires EIA for two lists of projects, which are shown in Appendix A.1. Annex I projects, for which EIA is required unconditionally, include crude oil refineries, large power stations, and disposal sites for hazardous wastes. Annex II projects may require EIA, depending on whether the competent authority — the authority that decides whether the projects should proceed or not — considers their impacts to be significant; examples of Annex II projects are agricultural developments, mineral extraction, and most roads. Directive 85/337 also lists the information that must be included in an EIA; this is shown in Appendix A.2.

The UK was initially reluctant to agree to standard EIA regulations, claiming that its existing planning system adequately prevented harmful developments (Wathern, 1988). It implemented Directive 85/337 through a number of items of secondary legislation. The Town and Country Planning (Assessment of Environmental Effects) Regulations 1988 cover about two-thirds of the relevant projects (Coles et al., 1992). Other projects that do not fall under the remit of these regulations, including afforestation, pipelines, harbour works, and projects in Scotland and Northern Ireland, are covered by 16 other regulations (DoE, 1988).

Five years after Directive 85/337 was adopted, several reports were prepared that discuss the current state and problems of both the directive and its implementation in the UK (eg. Coles and Tarling, 1991; CPRE, 1991; DoE, 1991c; Therivel, 1991). The directive has been criticized because it does not require EIA of projects that receive Parliamentary approval, defence projects, potable water treatment plants, most fish farms, wind power projects, leisure complexes, rural housing or fur farms. It gives no criteria to help the competent authorities to decide which Annex II (discretionary) projects require EIA. It requires public participation only once a formal application is made for a project, not throughout the project planning process. Its effectiveness is not adequately monitored. Finally, it does not require EIA for policies, plans and programmes.

The directive's implementation in the UK has also been criticized. First, the initial implementation of the directive through secondary legislation under the European Communities Act 1972 limited the application of EIA to only those projects specifically listed in the directive. This was remedied with the passing of the Planning and Compensation Act of 1991; the application of EIA to other projects such as golf courses, coastal protection works and windfarms is being considered by the Department of the Environment at the time of writing (DoE, 1992e).

Second, the criteria for determining whether an Annex II (reinterpreted in the UK as Schedule 2) project requires EIA are only in guidance form, leaving the final decision to the discretion of the competent authority. Local authorities appear to be unfamiliar with the regulations, and are not requiring EIA consistently; nor is the Department of the Environment (Gosling, 1990).

Third, some competent authorities – for instance the Department of Transport and the Forestry Commission – are both the project proponent and the competent authority for their EIAs. They can thus propose projects, prepare the relevant EIA, and decide whether the project should proceed or not: this is hardly conducive to unbiased decision-making.

The Department of Transport's requirements for EIA are particularly weak. Its Standard HD 018/88 relating to EIA contains the contentious statement that 'individual highway schemes do not have a significant effect on climatic factors and, in most cases, are unlikely to have significant effects on soil or water'.

The decision as to whether or not to discuss alternatives has been left virtually to the discretion of the developer. Only one quarter of EIAs consider alternatives (DoE, 1991c).

The quality of the resulting environmental impact statements has been very variable, with between one-third to two-thirds being unsatisfactory, depending on the reviewer and the time period reviewed; the standard of EISs is improving over time (Coles et al., 1992). There is no accepted standard for determining the quality of an EIS, although a few methodologies have been published and are gaining acceptance (Lee and Colley, 1990; Tomlinson, 1989).

There is no requirement to monitor the actual impacts caused by projects, and to compare them with the impacts predicted in EIAs. Finally, there is no official central repository for EISs.

In summary, EIA has become an accepted form of environmental management in many parts of the world. The less developed countries are less likely to require official EIAs owing to political and economic situations that make all but post-hoc reactive measures virtually impossible. In many industrialized countries EIA is well established, despite a range of factors limiting its effectiveness. Indeed, some countries are moving towards an extension of EIA to cover policies, plans and programmes as well as projects. This is expected to overcome some of the limitations of the existing EIA systems and is discussed in the next section.

1.3 The need for strategic environmental assessment

Strategic environmental assessment has so far been described as the application of environmental impact assessment at the level of policies, plans and programmes. More specifically, SEA can be defined as the formalized, systematic and comprehensive process of evaluating the environmental impacts of a policy, plan or programme and its alternatives, including the preparation of a written report on the findings of that evaluation, and using the findings in publicly accountable decision-making.

There are two broad approaches to SEA: one is to view it as an improvement on the existing process of 'project' EIA, and the other is as a way of 'trickling down' the objective of sustainability. This section briefly takes these approaches in turn to discuss the need for SEA.

SEA as an improvement over project EIA

In this book the term 'project' is taken to mean an individual development or other scheme, as distinct from a suite of schemes or a strategy for development of a particular type or in a particular region. It could be argued that EIA as practised, for instance in the UK under the EC Directive, operates at an even less strategic level than the 'project', since an EIA tends to be specific to a particular application for consent, several of which in fact may go to make up one 'project'. The broader interpretation, however, is followed here, such that the UK system is regarded as project-based.

Project EIA cannot in itself lead to comprehensive protection of the environment, for several reasons. First, it *reacts* to development proposals rather than anticipating them. Thus it cannot steer developments towards environmentally resilient locations or away from sensitive areas; it only allows for proposals to be accepted or rejected. EIA at a strategic level would allow a more proactive approach to be taken.

Second, it does not adequately consider the *cumulative impacts* of more than one project. Although EC Directive 85/337 and other similar legislation requires cumulative impacts to be considered in an EIA, in practice this is very rarely done. For instance, Chapter 6 shows that the cumulative impacts of development on heathland are not addressed in EISs. Cumulative impacts can take several forms:

- the *additive impacts* of developments that do not require EIA according to existing legislation, such as small-scale projects, defence-related projects and many agricultural projects;

- *synergistic impacts* where several projects' total impacts exceed the sum of their individual impacts. For instance, in the presence of sunlight, nitrogen oxides and hydrocarbons may combine to form photochemical oxidants, which have impacts over and above those of only the nitrogen oxides and hydrocarbons;

- *threshold/saturation impacts* where the environment may be resilient up to a certain level and then becomes rapidly degraded. An example would be a stream that is self-purifying up to a given level of pollutants and then loses its self-purification ability;

- *induced and indirect impacts* where one development project can stimulate secondary developments and infrastructure. For instance, an airport could trigger applications for hotels and car rental developments. A new motorway may provide the focus for a whole new range of developments, from hypermarkets to new towns to service stations; and

- *time-crowded or space-crowded impacts*, where the environment does not have the time or space to recover from one impact before it is subject to the next one. An example would be a forestry operation with an overly-rapid rotation period, which could cause soil productivity to fall.

The consideration of cumulative impacts in project EIA is often limited by the lack of knowledge concerning other development proposals, and lack of control over these proposals (Montgomery, 1990). EIA at a more strategic level would allow for these impacts to be better addressed because of its position at an earlier stage in decision-making and its consideration of a wider range of actions over a greater area.

Third, project EIA only addresses *alternatives* to the proposed project in a limited manner. This is partly due to the lack of guidance and emphasis generally given to alternatives in EIA legislation, and partly due to the fact that in many cases a project's details are already drawn up quite specifically, with irreversible decisions taken, by the time an EIA is prepared. This problem could be partly but not wholly addressed with a more stringent system of project EIA: in the US, for instance, it has for a long time been a requirement that EIAs must: 'rigorously explore and objectively evaluate all reasonable alternatives, and for alternatives which were eliminated from detailed study, briefly discuss the reasons for their having been eliminated' (USCEQ, 1978). However, this still does not allow for an assessment of alternatives in earlier stages of planning, as would be provided for by SEA.

The *measures for mitigation of impacts* proposed in project EIAs are similarly limited. Mitigation measures can be viewed in some senses as a form of alternative. Like other alternatives, the types of mitigation measures used, how they are applied, and their effectiveness are all affected by actions taken previously. Mitigation measures are often added on to a project only after the major decisions – location, type, scale – have been made. It is even questionable whether in practice mitigation measures are used to counter the most negative impacts of a project, or whether they are simply used for those impacts that can be most easily ameliorated; further monitoring studies would be needed to determine this.

The *timescale* for preparing a project EIA is often determined by other factors, particularly financial constraints and the timing of planning applications. As a result, many project EIAs are undertaken in a compressed period of time, often within a few months. This limits the amount of baseline data that can be collected, and the quality of analysis that can be undertaken. EIA expertise is often brought into a project too late to make an adequate contribution. A strategic approach would enable relevant experts to be more fully involved at early planning stages. Finally, the amount and type of *public consultation* undertaken in project EIA may be limited for similar reasons (Contant and Wiggins, 1991; Montgomery, 1990).

The relative significance of these problems will depend on the type of project involved and the place where it is to be located.

SEA as a means of implementing sustainability

SEA is also needed as a way of implementing the concept of sustainability. Sustainability goes beyond weighing up impacts or preventing environmental damage of individual projects, or even of PPPs. It has been defined as meaning that:

> the environment should be protected in such a condition and to such a degree that environmental capacities (the ability of the environment to perform its various functions) are maintained over time: at least at levels sufficient to avoid future catastrophe, and at most at levels which give future generations the opportunity to enjoy an equal measure of environmental consumption (Jacobs, 1991).

Sustainability – or the version that seems in many quarters to be more palatable, sustainable development – has become accepted as the goal of many environmental policies, especially since the Brundtland Commission's report of 1987 (WCED, 1987). However, its actual implementation is considerably more problematic. In theory, sustainability requires a proactive approach that encompasses a wide range of human activities and environmental factors. Sustainability would need to be made an intrinsic part of all policies, and then 'trickled down' through plans, programmes, and ultimately to projects. However, there are many practical problems to this, which will be further addressed in Chapter 7.

The Netherlands appears to have progressed the official implementation of sustainability further than other countries. In response to the Brundtland Commission's report (WCED, 1987) on sustainable development, the Netherlands' State Institute for Health and Environment prepared a 1988 report entitled 'Concern for Tomorrow', which broadly establishes what changes would be needed to achieve sustainability. For instance, the report noted that a reduction of 70-90 per cent for a wide range of discharges and emissions would be needed. It also noted that such reductions would require changes of consumption and production patterns as well as so-called 'end-of-pipe' techniques. The National Environmental Policy Plan (NEPP) of 1989 and its update (NEPP-plus) of 1990, which define the Netherlands' environmental strategy for the next decade, subsequently aimed at achieving the changes proposed in 'Concern for Tomorrow'. A major component of the NEPP is the requirement to carry out an EIA for all policies, plans and programmes that have significant environmental impacts; the Dutch system of SEA is discussed in Chapter 3.

In summary, EIA of projects is effective only in a minimal and remedial way if the strategic decisions that ultimately generate the projects are intrinsically environmentally harmful, or are progressed without regard to the harm which they might have. SEA would not only overcome the worst limitations of the existing system of project EIA, but would also be a proactive step towards attaining sustainability.

1.4 Trends in approaches to environmental issues: links with strategic environmental assessment

This section reviews some recent and likely future trends in approaches to environmental issues, and identifies links between SEA and these trends. Some major recent environmental initiatives are summarized in boxes as examples of these trends. Other examples from the UK are given in the text, but the trends themselves are global.

Approaches to environmental problems have evolved greatly since the first pollution control laws were passed about 130 years ago (Ball and Bell, 1991). Those early laws were meant to stop serious but localized harm to human health from pollution. The post-war years saw a marked increase in the quantity and variety of pollutants, and later – with such incidents as the heavy metal poisonings in Japan in the 1960s, and toxic waste contamination problems in the US in the 1970s – a growing realization of the long-term and cumulative consequences of these pollutants. The 1970s saw a surge in the development of technical solutions to these problems, including flue gas desulphurization, catalytic converters, and various techniques for treating and disposing of hazardous wastes.

However, it is only in the last decade that the intrinsic interdependence of the economy and the environment, the global scale of environmental problems, and the necessity to consider environmental issues on an institutional as well as a technical level have been fully acknowledged. The 1987 meeting of the Brundtland Commission (see Box 1.1), and the 1992 Earth Summit in Rio de Janeiro (see Box 1.2) were both major forums for discussing how environmental issues could be dealt with at a global level in an economic, equitable and holistic way. Further information on the evolution and present state of approaches to the environment can be found, for instance, in Ball and Bell (1991), Barrett and Therivel (1991), CEC (1992), McCormick (1991), OECD (1991), Owens and Owens (1992), and WCED (1987).

Box 1.1 Brundtland Commission 1987

The World Commission on Environment and Development (the 'Brundtland Commission') was established in 1983 with the aim of setting 'a global agenda for change'. Its remit was to examine critical issues in environment and development and formulate realistic proposals for dealing with them; propose new forms of international cooperation concerning these issues; and raise the levels of understanding and commitment to action. Its report of 1987, *Our Common Future* (WCED, 1987), put forward such an agenda.

Our Common Future is based on the concept that it is impossible to separate economic development issues from environmental issues. It sees poverty as a major cause and effect of global environmental problems, and argues that environmental conditions can only be improved through the satisfaction of human needs and aspirations, and a growth in national incomes.

It proposes sustainable development – ensuring that the needs of the present are met without compromising the ability of future generations to meet their needs – as the way forward. To promote sustainable development, it suggests that greater emphasis should be placed on multilateralism and global cooperation, social issues, equity, and the reorientation of technology and institutional framework to take greater account of the environment.

Internationalization

In the last decade, the global nature of many of our environmental problems has become acknowledged, with increasing information about issues such as global warming, the depletion of the ozone layer, the destruction of great areas of rainforest, and the possible effects of the smoke plumes caused by the Gulf War. The climate in more developed countries has been shown to be affected by the actions of less developed countries, just as the reserves of natural resources in less developed countries are affected by consumer demand in more developed countries.

Unfortunately, the acknowledgement of these links has not simplified negotiations concerning technical and economic transfers from more developed countries in return for greater environmental sensitivity by the less developed (see Box 1.2). However, one can expect more, and more successful, negotiations to take place in the future that will establish clear international goals concerning environmental issues. In turn, this will require the establishment of more reliable and comparable national databases on the environment (CEC, 1992; OECD, 1991).

***Box 1.2* Earth Summit 1992**

The United Nations Conference on Environment and Development (the 'Earth Summit') of June 1992 addressed issues of economic and environmental interaction and distribution, in an attempt to progress towards sustainable development. It was attended by representatives of more than 170 countries, but despite this large showing and high expectations, it resulted in relatively minor agreements:

- a treaty on climate change, including a non-binding proposal for developed nations to stabilize their emissions of greenhouse gases at 1990 levels by the year 2000;

- a treaty on the need for countries to protect biodiversity within their borders. The US did not sign this because it felt that the treaty compromised its biotechnology industry;

- the Rio Declaration, a set of 27 non-binding principles on environmental and development issues;

- Agenda 21, an 800-page non-binding action plan for achieving sustainable development;

- a proposed UN Commission on sustainable development;

- increases of nearly £1 billion/year in Third World aid. Implementation of Agenda 21 would cost about £40 billion/year; and

- a set of non-binding principles for conserving and rationally exploiting forests.

These agreements were the result, put simply, of negotiations between richer nations, which wanted to maintain their own status quo while at the same time requiring poor nations to preserve their environmental assets, and poorer nations, which wanted financial and technical resources to help them to carry out this preservation (*Guardian*, June 1992; *Independent*, June 1992).

Integration and institutional coherence

Another trend in the approach to environmental issues is the increasing integration of environmental policies and regulations, and the growing coherence of institutional structures for dealing with the environment (this is counteracted to some degree by their continued proliferation). Environmental issues are inherently difficult to compartmentalise, but until recently environmental legislation focused on individual media (air, water, soil) or pollutants. This artificial simplification, and the fact that environmental issues have only recently been considered as part of the political agenda, has meant that the institutional and legislative structures for deal-

---

Box 1.3 UK Environmental Protection Act 1990

The Environmental Protection Act 1990 is made up of nine parts that respectively address pollution control, waste on land, statutory nuisances and clean air, litter, radioactive substances, genetically modified organisms, nature conservation, miscellaneous and general items. Of these, the most relevant to this book are Part I (pollution control) and Part II (waste on land).

Part I requires the application of Integrated Pollution Control (IPC) by Her Majesty's Inspectorate of Pollution (HMIP), and Air Pollution Control (APC) by local authorities. IPC applies to about 5,500 complex industrial operations (either new or existing), while APC applies to about 11,000 manufacturing processes and 10-15,000 waste oil burners. In both cases, process operators must obtain authorization to start or continue operating the process, based on a staggered timetable starting in April 1991.

IPC requires operators of the processes to show to the HMIP that they use the Best Available Techniques Not Entailing Excessive Cost (BATNEEC) to prevent, minimize, or render harmless releases of prescribed substances; and, where a process is likely to involve releases into more than one environmental medium, operators must show that they use the Best Practicable Environmental Option (BPEO) to minimize pollution to the environment as a whole (releases to air, water and soil). APC requires only proof that BATNEEC has been used.

The HMIP and local authorities must set up public registers of authorizations and related information; and they must recover the costs of the schemes through a fee system.

Part II requires local authorities to separate the functions of waste disposal and waste regulation; waste disposal is now to be done by 'arm's length' (i.e. from the regulators) or private firms, while local authorities remain responsible for regulation. Anyone collecting, transporting or disposing of waste must now obtain authorization for their activities. Most importantly, Part II imposes a 'Duty of Care' on any holder of waste to transfer it only to an authorized person and to dispose of it correctly. The waste must be accompanied 'from cradle to grave' by a form stating its origin, subsequent handling and composition.

---

ing with these issues have developed in an ad hoc, incremental, and ineffective way (McCormick, 1991).

The limitations of this approach are being recognized and remedied. Environmental legislation is being developed that attempts to minimize the impact of developments on the environment as a whole; the UK's Environmental Protection Act of 1990 (see Box 1.3), for instance, requires that industrial processes that are likely to involve releases into more than one medium use techniques that cause the least overall impact on the environment as a whole (Ball and Bell, 1991; Slater, 1992). New legislation is beginning to require the consideration of indirect and cumulative impacts of development projects as well as their direct impacts; pollution from diffuse as well as point sources; and exposure to multiple as well as individual sources of pollution.

In parallel, institutional structures are being reshuffled and rationalized. Privatisation is formalizing the separation between the producer of goods and services (clean water, waste disposal, space on railway lines) and the regulating authority responsible for ensuring the quality of these goods and services (see Box 1.3 for an example). The responsibility for environmental protection is becoming increasingly formalized and centralized, as can be seen in the formation of Her Majesty's Inspectorate of Pollution in 1987, the National Rivers Authority in 1989, and the European Environmental Agency in the future (Ball and Bell, 1991; Owens and Owens, 1991). While in the past environmental protection in the UK was to some eyes characterized by consensus, consultation, and discretion by the enforcing authorities, more recently it has become considerably more formalized, confrontational, and prone to legal challenge (McCormick, 1991).

Prevention of environmental harm, the need for data, and the role of uncertainty

Over time, approaches to environmental issues have evolved from reacting to problems after they arose to anticipating problems and attempting to deal with them before they occur. Recent, more strategic approaches include EIA, SEA and (to an extent) environmental auditing, which respectively aim to minimize the environmental impacts of proposed development projects, proposed PPPs, and existing developments.

However, predictive approaches require considerably more information about environmental systems than do reactive approaches. Little is known about the causes, impacts and solutions for many environmental problems; areas where further research is needed include ecological carrying capacity, biodiversity, the marine environment, risks of long-term pollution, criteria for impact significance, and the environmental impacts of economic and sectoral policies (OECD, 1991).

Various organizations are calling for more, and better organized, data on the environment (CEC, 1992; OECD, 1991). Methods of remote sensing and geographical information systems are being developed for the rapid collection, statistical analysis and comparison of such data. The need to harmonize the data of different countries so as to make them comparable, for instance by establishing agreed environmental indicators and methods for monitoring them, has been stressed (OECD, 1991).

However, the present lack of data is making it necessary to plan for uncertainty, be it uncertainty about the future state of the environment, future development projects, or the impact that the latter will have on the former. Techniques for dealing with uncertainty include the use of pilot projects and contingency plans, sensitivity testing, and risk minimization to avoid the worst possible outcomes. Recent approaches to environmental issues have been incorporating these techniques (eg. DoE, 1991a; WCED, 1987).

Valuation of environmental goods

Methods for determining the true environmental costs of products to consumers received a great deal of interest in the 1960s and 1970s, but declined in the 1980s as critics emphasized their practical limitations. Recently, market-based instruments have once again been promoted by some as the least costly and most effective way of protecting the environment. Assigning the true values to environmental goods, and 'charging' them to the consumer, is expected to sensitize consumers and producers to the use of natural resources and the production of pollution, thereby (it is hoped) leading to reduced environmental harm. New techniques are emerging for assigning correct values to environmental goods (e.g. hedonic price methods, travel cost methods) as well as for charging the consumer (e.g. carbon tax, packaging laws). Recent studies on the valuation of environmental goods include those of Dixon et al. (1986), Pearce et al. (1989), and Winpenny (1991).

Equity and public participation

There is growing acknowledgement that environmental sustainability is intrinsically connected with the notion of equity, both temporal (between generations) and spatial (within generations): sustainability implies passing on environmental resources undiminished to future generations, but achieving sustainability also requires the present-day international cooperation of a wide range of interest groups (WCED, 1987). Studies on existing levels and uses of resources, appropriate discount rates, and the possibility of trading human-made resources for natural resources are contributing, albeit slowly, to achieving intergenerational equity. Discussions such as those at the Earth Summit concerning technology transfers, sovereignty over natural resources, and Third World debt are, again slowly, attempting to tackle intragenerational equity.

Finally, there is increasing recognition of the need for greater public accessibility to environmental data, more public education concerning environmental issues, and more public participation in environmental decision-making. A major side-benefit to all concerned of EIA, for instance, has been the fact that it allows the public to participate more in the decision-making process. The UK Environmental Protection Act 1990 requires local authorities and HMIP to set up publicly accessible pollution registers. One can also expect more citizen lawsuits on environmental grounds in the future.

The role of SEA

SEA is in many ways a prototype of this new approach to environmental issues. It requires institutions to consider the consequences of a range of actions early on in the planning process, to choose the most appropriate action on environmental as well as socio-economic grounds, and to minimize any remaining environmental impacts. It is thus characterized by its strategic nature and its emphasis on preventing environmental damage. SEA requires environmental data as the basis for its predictions, as well as greater institutional cooperation to collect the data and to make consistent predictions; for instance, it encourages the coordination of PPPs for energy, transport and land use. By requiring planning decisions to be made in a more rational and open way, SEA is likely to promote both equity and public participation.

Methodologies for SEA are not yet well-developed. However, they are likely to include elements of cost-benefit and monetary valuation. They will also need to cope with high levels of uncertainty; they are thus likely to encourage the development of precautionary methodologies as well as the collection and interpretation of baseline environmental data. This is discussed further in Appendix C.

SEA has close links with a number of other environmental initiatives. National environmental policies, such as the Netherlands' NEPP of 1989, the US National Environmental Policy Act of 1969 and, to a lesser extent, the UK White Paper on the Environment of 1990 (see Box 1.4), establish national environmental objectives and ways of achieving these objectives; they can require the preparation of SEAs. The environmental data collected by local authorities for environmental audits could also be used in future SEAs. EIAs of individual projects could take place within a framework set up by an SEA. Comprehensive plans for particular habitats or sectors, such as the UK House of Commons' recent proposals for comprehensive management of coastlines (House of Commons Environment Committee, 1992), could evolve from or within a system of SEA.

1.5 Conclusions

This chapter has shown that EIA of projects is widely carried out, but that its effectiveness is constrained by socio-political and economic factors. It is also limited by the fact that it generally applies only to the lowest, project tier of assessment; this in turn is heavily influenced by the higher strategic tiers that give rise to the projects.

SEA is one way of overcoming limitations of the existing system of project EIA. It could allow the principle of sustainability to be implemented in a phased way from policies to plans, programmes and the projects. It would also provide a focus for other approaches to environmental issues; generally, these approaches are becoming more integrated, holistic and forward-looking. Chapter 2 focuses on SEA as a form of policy appraisal.

Box 1.4 UK White Paper on the Environment 1990

The White Paper on the Environment of 1990 (SoS, 1990) was hailed by the then Secretary of State, Chris Patten, as 'the first really comprehensive statement of government policy on the environment, ranging from the street corner to the stratosphere, from human health to endangered species'. The paper explains the current state of the environment in the UK under the following headings:

Part I.   The Government's Approach (first principles; the environment in Britain; Europe; Britain and the world environment)

Part II.   The Greenhouse Effect (Britain and global warming)

Part III.   Town and Country (land use, countryside and wildlife, towns and cities, the heritage)

Part IV.   Pollution Control (Britain's approach to pollution control; air; water; hazardous substances and genetically modified organisms; waste and recycling; nuclear power and radioactive waste; noise)

Part V.   Awareness and Organization (knowledge; education and training; institutions and consultation)

Part VI.   Scotland, Wales and Northern Ireland (the environment in Wales, the environment in Scotland, the environment in Northern Ireland)

The White Paper sets out more than 350 proposals for action in these areas. Most of these proposals are phrased more as general directions that the government would wish to follow rather than clear, quantative objectives to be attained. For instance, the government will '*call for* improved standards of air quality monitoring', '*promote* wider use of combined heat and power', and '*support* the development of forestry initiatives' [emphasis added].

One consultancy's summary for businesses of the White Paper began:

> The White Paper holds no terrors for business. There is nothing of a concrete nature in the 291 pages which will affect business in a manner that was not already evident from existing policy and legal initiatives. The White Paper thus lacks the 'strategic' impact that is normally associated with such documents (Linklaters and Paines, 1990).

Notes

1. Although the term 'environmental assessment' is generally used in the UK for this process, the authors feel that 'environmental impact assessment' (as used in the US and elsewhere) is a more accurate description.

2:

Strategic environmental assessment and policy appraisal

This chapter develops in more detail some of the arguments for extending environmental impact assessment from projects to the policies, plans and programmes that give rise to those projects or provide their context. It examines the issue against the background of more general concepts of policy appraisal and evaluation. As was discussed in Chapter 1, SEA can be seen as the extension to an earlier stage in the decision-making process of project EIA as more commonly practised: the arguments for assessing the impacts of a policy or programme before it becomes manifested in projects themselves need reviewing in the context of a more general discussion of the policy process. The extent to which policies, plans and programmes form a simple progressive framework for addressing these matters is also discussed.

2.1 Strategic environmental assessment in UK policy-making

In the UK, the policy process has been characterized by a lack of strategic vision or formal procedures for appraising strategic decisions. Traditional British practices of policy formulation and implementation have often been described as ad hoc and discretionary, without provision or opportunity for adequate review of the wider implications of policy adoption and strategic choice (O'Riordan and Hey, 1976). This has been the case in both national economic planning and national land use or development planning. The abandonment of forward national planning in the 1970s contrasts, for instance, with the trend observed in Japan, which has instituted a system of plans for both the national economy and physical development: national economic plans are complemented by the spatial dimension of comprehensive national development plans (Barrett and Therivel, 1991). This relationship is illustrated in Box 2.1.

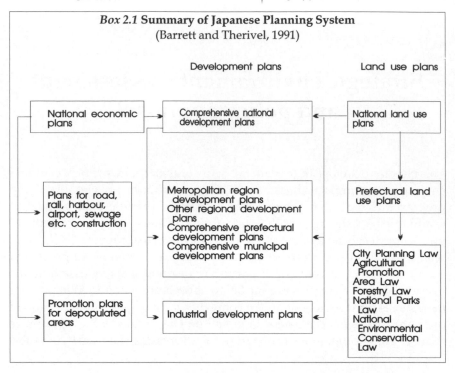

Box 2.1 Summary of Japanese Planning System
(Barrett and Therivel, 1991)

Moreover, environmental policy in the UK, even where it is seen as a policy arena in its own right, suffers from this aversion to long-term, strategic planning. It is characterized by both its piecemeal and pragmatic approaches to problems as they have arisen (such as acid rain), and by a process of incorporation, whereby affected interests are closely involved with the formulation of new environmental initiatives or regulations (McCormick, 1991).

The result of the incremental nature of British policy-making, and of (for the most part) the lack of an identifiable environmental policy as such, has been to inhibit the opportunities for incorporating environmental impact assessment into policy-making and decision-making. However, as EIA has become more accepted in the US and elsewhere, arguments have been advanced for introducing procedures to ensure that environmental implications are considered at the policy-making stage, in which new initiatives such as legislation and new government policies are assessed, as well as major public development proposals or projects (O'Riordan and Hey, 1976).

The case for strategic environmental assessment has been advanced in the 1980s by a number of agencies, for both national policy formulation and for the activities of international organizations such as the World Bank or the European Communities (Wood and Djeddour, 1991). The European Commission included commitments to the eventual extension of EIA to its own policies and programmes in its Fourth Action Programme on the Environment, and has repeated this commitment in the Fifth Action Programme (discussed in more detail in Chapter 3).

In the UK, the recent report of the Standing Advisory Committee on Trunk Road Assessment concluded that

> the environmental effects of road building and road traffic, across the full spectrum, cannot... all be reflected at one single level of decision-making, and certainly not just at the level of scheme assessment. If all effects are to be taken into account in Government decisions, the appropriate environmental appraisal must underlie every stage in the hierarchy of decisions, from the making of national and regional policy downwards (SACTRA, 1992).

2.2 Strategic environmental assessment as policy appraisal

SEA has been advocated by many individuals and government agencies as an improvement on the existing limited system of project EIA. But other factors have also contributed to the promotion of systematic review of the environmental consequences of government policies and activities. First, there has been an increased awareness of the global and international dimensions of government activity at all levels, and of the complex interaction between the economy and the environment. Second, there has been a long-standing concern over the opportunities available for the public and interested parties to participate in discussions about need and alternatives in the policy-formulation stage. Third, these factors have coincided with moves within government itself to undertake more systematic appraisal of different policy options, to improve decision-making and accountability by considering the costs and benefits of a proposed policy, and by comparing the different measures needed to implement it, including the financial, social and environmental implications.

For instance, the idea of a tiered or nested sequence of assessment of the different levels of government action has been linked also with broader concerns about the opportunities given to Parliament, its committees, or to the public, to review the wider consequences of government policy. The possible scope for linking SEA with the opportunities then existing for public hearings or inquiries was suggested by O'Riordan and Hey (1976) in the proposal illustrated in Box 2.2. A number of reports and inquiries in the 1980s took up this theme, and challenged the opportunities given in the traditional public inquiry system for discussion and review of major issues of government policy, especially those of need (Outer Circle Policy Unit, 1979; Glasson and Elson, 1987).

This distinction between issues of overall need and more site-specific issues was also taken up by the House of Commons Environment Select Committee in its 1986 report on planning appeals and major public inquiries (HoC Environment Committee, 1986). The committee's investigations were prompted by concern over the major public inquiries for the Sizewell B pressurized water reactor (PWR), Stansted Airport, and the Vale of

Belvoir coal mine: specifically the length and cost of these inquiries, the role and status of third parties, and the suitability of such inquiries for examining, or even on occasion determining, central government policy. In their conclusion, the Select Committee recommended that 'wherever possible, national policy should be clearly determined and laid down by government prior to a planning inquiry on a major development that should take place within the context of such policy'. The committee considered that policy, for instance for radioactive waste disposal or for PWRs generally, could well be resolved at a preliminary or primary stage inquiry.

The government, however, did not accept the committee's recommendations on this matter. Accordingly, the inquiry into the application for a second PWR at Hinkley Point (Hinkley C) was given no specific remit to discuss issues of need and alternatives, which were held to have been fully examined at the Sizewell B inquiry. Nevertheless, the objections of the Consortium of Local Authorities to the proposal inevitably raised these issues, and the Inspector in his report devoted considerable attention to discussing these questions, as well as the site-specific aspects of the proposal (Barnes, 1990).

The controversy over the system of major public inquiries was overtaken, towards the end of the 1980s, by the British government's apparent 'conversion' to the environment as a political issue. The reasons for that change of heart, both personal and political, domestic and international, have been fully documented elsewhere (Lowe and Flynn, 1989; McCormick, 1991; and Webb, 1991).

One of the specific consequences of the new attention in government to environmental issues was the undertaking made by the then Secretary of State for the Environment at the Annual Conference of the Conservative Party to produce a White Paper on the environment. The resulting document *This Common Inheritance* (SoS, 1990) was designed to offer a comprehensive statement of the government's record and intentions on many areas of environmental concern, from the global to the local, with some commitments for new legislation, regulations or budgetary allocations (see Box 1.4). It also offered an opportunity for a review of the way in which environmental concerns were integrated into government policy-making at an institutional level. Chapter 18 of the White Paper is devoted to institutional change and government activity, and states that:

> During the preparation of this White Paper, each Government Department has reviewed the environmental implications of its existing policies and considered changes to them. Where this has resulted in proposals for change, these are included in the relevant chapters. To build on that exercise, and to ensure that the environmental implications of decisions are fully considered beforehand, the Government has carried out a review of the way in which the costs and benefits of environmental issues are assessed within Government. The review has looked at the range of analysis which is available on environmental costs and benefits, recognizing the need for an integrated approach which takes account of all the

consequences of a measure for the environment, favourable and unfavourable. It has concluded that there is scope for a more systematic approach within Government to the appraisal of the environmental costs and benefits before decisions are taken.

Guidelines on the more systematic approach promised in the White Paper were published as *Policy Appraisal and the Environment* (Department of Environment, 1991a). The document is reviewed in Chapter 3, which points out its limitations as a form of SEA; but it can be seen as a further contribution by the UK government to formalizing its internal processes of policy appraisal. The Treasury had previously published guidance on policy evaluation (which it defined as the process of examining a policy in the light of what has happened during or after the operation of the policy) (HM Treasury, 1988), and guidance on integrating economic appraisal into central government for both capital and current expenditure (HM Treasury, 1991).

There is thus a considerable weight of academic and policy-making opinion that points to the need for an assessment of the implications of policy and alternatives at a strategic stage. The arguments for SEA can be summarized as offering an improvement on the existing case-by-case reactive system of project EIA, helping to put principles of sustainability into operation, giving an opportunity for public involvement in policy formulation, and ensuring systematic appraisal of choices.

These principles can be expressed as *objectives for a system of SEA*:

- to ensure the full consideration of alternative policy options, including the 'do-nothing' option, at an early time when an agency has greater flexibility;

- to enable consistency to be developed across different policy sectors, especially where trade-offs need to be made between objectives;

- to ensure that the cumulative, indirect or secondary impacts of diverse multiple activities are considered, including their unintended consequences;

- to enable adverse environmental impacts to be anticipated and hence avoided or prevented;

- to ensure that the environmental impact of policies that do not have an overt environmental dimension is assessed;

- to obviate the needless reassessment of issues and impacts at project level where such issues could more effectively be dealt with at a strategic level, and offer time and cost savings;

- to provide a publicly available and accountable decision-making framework;

- to ensure that environmental principles such as sustainability and the precautionary principle are integrated into the development, appraisal and selection of policy options;

- to give proper place to environmental considerations in decision-making *vis-à-vis* economic and social concerns, given that in some contexts they may be traded off against each other.

2.3 The tiered approach to environmental impact assessment

The suggestion that EIA should be carried out in 'overlapping tiers' has been promoted both by academics (e.g. O'Riordan and Hey, 1976) and by government agencies (eg. State of California, 1986). Box 2.2 illustrates one possibility for a system of overlapping EIA tiers.

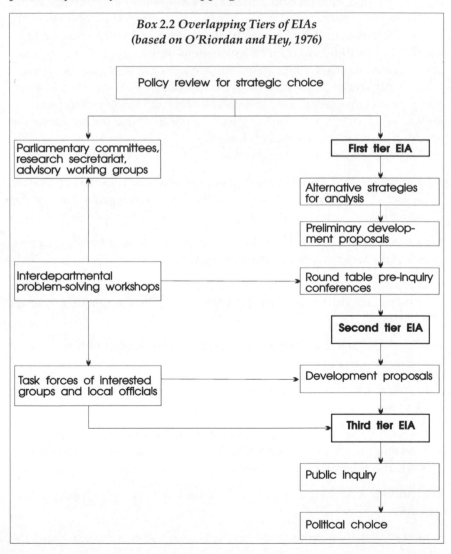

Box 2.2 Overlapping Tiers of EIAs
(based on O'Riordan and Hey, 1976)

government agencies (eg. State of California, 1986). Box 2.2 illustrates one possibility for a system of overlapping EIA tiers.

References to the importance and advisability of a tiered approach to assessment imply that the different stages in the formulation and implementation of a policy nest within one another, and that policies, plans and programmes are each a distinct stage of the process. Conventional definitions are that *policies* are 'the Government's objectives and the preferred means for trying to achieve them' (HM Treasury, 1988) while *programmes* or *plans* are sets of related activities and expenditure that give effect to

---

Box 2.3 The Common Agricultural Policy of the EC
(RSPB, 1988)

The objectives of the CAP: Article 39 of the Treaty of Rome

The objectives of the common agricultural policy shall be:

(a) to increase agricultural productivity by promoting technical progress and by ensuring the rational development of agricultural production and the optimum utilisation of the factors of production, in particular labour;

(b) thus to ensure a fair standard of living for the agricultural community, in particular by increasing the individual earnings of persons engaged in agriculture;

(c) to stabilise markets;

(d) to assure the availability of supplies;

(e) to ensure that supplies reach consumers at reasonable prices.

The CAP is **funded by** the European Agricultural Guarantee and Guidance Fund:

The Guarantee Sector	*The Guidance Sector*
This raises farm incomes by price guarantees, consumer and producer subsidies, or direct intervention.	This is designed to improve farm structures or to protect less well-favoured farms through grant aid for capital investment.

Examples of **activities** stimulated by the policy include the shift to cereal production away from livestock, or to sheepmeat within the livestock sector, and the effects of grant aid for the reseeding of grassland, fencing to improve control of stock and new buildings for livestock enterprises. Environmental impact assessment does not occur, if at all, until this last stage of capital projects.

policy (including policy areas with little or no public expenditure). Programmes may in turn be composed of *projects*, discrete activities usually at specific locations, and often requiring capital expenditure (HM Treasury, 1988; DoE, 1991a). Plans can also have a more specific meaning in the context of land-use or physical development planning. Whatever the precise definition given, the implication is that projects are undertaken within a programme, which in turn is the specific expression of a policy.

An example would be the Common Agricultural Policy (CAP) of the EC, whose objectives are set out in the Treaty of Rome, Article 39, and relate to productivity, the living standards of farmers, and market characteristics (RSPB, 1988). The policy is implemented through the European Agricultural Guarantee and Guidance Fund, which encourages particular practices or developments through the system of price support and grant aid for capital investment. The sequence of policy through to project is illustrated in Box 2.3.

A UK example of the different stages of the policy process is the sequence of events leading to the construction of a trunk road (illustrated in Box 2.4). The government sets out its policy objectives, for instance to relieve congestion or promote economic prosperity, in the White Papers on roads, which then interact with local initiatives or concerns to give rise to suggested schemes. After a series of initial studies of the options, the schemes are incorporated into the national roads programme, but environmental impact assessment does not occur until the stage of selection of the preferred route.

The examples of policies and programmes given in the boxes illustrate cases where policy is given expression through specific, capital projects. But policies as general aspirations or statements of intent also include non-sectoral initiatives, which do not necessarily convert into capital projects, such as fiscal policy, and policies such as privatization, which require specific programmes of legislation for their implementation, but may not lead directly to on-the-ground development proposals. Appraisal at the policy formulation level is even more important for these 'meta-policies' because they are not converted into discrete projects for which a conventional EIA may be done (DoE, 1991a).

While recognising, therefore, that the terms 'policy', 'plan' and 'programme' are not always precisely distinguished, they can all be seen as part of the allocation and distribution of public resources through the policy process (Wood, 1991).

2.4 Concepts in policy appraisal

The definitions of policies, plans and programmes given above imply a clear distinction from projects or schemes, and imply a hierarchical, or even chronological, sequence of the policy process. This conception, however,

---

Box 2.4 Stages in the evolution of trunk road schemes
(based on SACTRA, 1992; and Department of Transport, 1992a)

The **objectives** of national policy for roads are set out in the Department of Transport's report on *The Government's Expenditure Plans for Transport 1992-93 To 1994-95 Cm1907*:

* to assist economic growth by reducing transport costs;

* to improve the environment by removing through traffic from unsuitable roads in towns and villages;

* to enhance road safety by building safer roads, securing improvement in the safety of vehicles, and encouraging better behaviour by drivers;

* to obtain full and safe use of the existing road network by pedestrians, cyclists, passengers, and drivers and to maintain and manage it in a cost-effective manner.

The first three **policy** aims were stated in the White Paper *Roads for Prosperity* Cm 693 (Department of Transport, 1989), which announced an expanded motorway and trunk road programme, and were repeated in the report *Trunk Roads, England: Into the 1990s* (Department of Transport 1990), which gave more detail of the timing of the schemes announced in the White Paper. Route or Scheme Identification Studies examine whether there is a need for a road-requiring solution.

Programme entry, requiring ministerial approval, is normally made in the White Paper or Roads Report.

Identification of possible routes includes initial surveys and appraisals (including cost-benefit analysis and the scheme's first framework) prior to public consultation, which leads to an announcement by the Secretary of State of the **preferred route**. Detailed design and survey work leads to the Order Publication Report, which includes a framework incorporating revised assessments, prior to the publication of Draft Line Orders. It is at this stage that the environmental impact statement under EC Directive 85/337 is published. A Public Inquiry may be held, on which the Inspector will report to the Secretary of State. The Secretary of State's decision, if favourable, leads to works commitment approval, invitation to tender, letting of contracts, and start of construction.

---

has been challenged by academic and political commentators. Problems with the concepts of hierarchies and of boundaries to the policy process have been a theme of policy analysis since the 1950s, with an emphasis on the complexity and open-endedness of policy definition and formulation. The language of ends and means that we use to describe the process is said to disguise its complexity and non-linearity, and our tools of analysis are held to be inadequate to reflect the lack of temporal or political limits to the policy process (Smith, 1976; Hogwood, 1987). There is not always a stage at which government determines public policy, a point recognised by central government. For instance, the Environment Committee in its report on major inquiries, referred to above, quoted the view of a witness: 'The fact remains that policy itself does not stand still and the moment at which a particular proposal comes forward is not always by any means of the Secretary of State's choosing and therefore it may be inevitable that policy issues are not as precise as many people would wish' (HoC Environment Committee, 1986).

Policy appraisal will also be difficult where the outcomes of policies or programmes are unintended, and the effects of the policy cannot be predicted. This may particularly characterize the environmental consequences of policy decisions (Wathern et al, 1988).

Even supposing that, for the purposes of appraisal, it is useful to assume that there are distinct and discrete stages in the policy process, and that boundaries to the influences on policy formulation, and the outcomes of policy, can be defined, there are still difficulties with the notion of a hierarchical process where policies are seen as 'higher-order' actions. Much of the work on policy in action has shown the importance of the implementation stage in interpreting and thereby also itself formulating policy (Barrett and Fudge, 1981). An example is the evolution of air pollution policy in the UK. Its implementation has been characterized by the features of discretion, voluntary compliance and negotiation between the regulators and the regulated, which have largely determined the policy in practice (McCormick, 1991).

The implications of the complexity of policy decisions are spelt out by Ham and Hill (1984). They describe a network or web of decisions over time, rather than one identifiable occasion on which policy is made, and the possibility that policy itself is more likely to be a series of decisions than a single one. The dynamic nature of the policy process means issues are likely to be redefined throughout the process, and it may be that a series of actions, even if not formally sanctioned by a decision, constitute policy. Moreover, the lack of an explicit policy decision may itself amount to a policy, and may therefore require analysis. These difficulties may be particularly acute in analysing the impacts of a policy, where both the intended and unintended consequences require assessment.

There are therefore conceptual problems in undertaking policy appraisal and in prescribing for that appraisal to be undertaken either as part of the formulation of the policy, or as an academic exercise. There are also difficulties in the practice of internal policy review within government: Gray and Jenkins, writing in the early 1980s, bemoaned the change in emphasis in the early part of the decade in which policy analysis had lost its strategic focus, being characterized by 'ad hoc reviews of operational efficiency with the primary focus on costs' (Gray and Jenkins, 1983). Throughout the 1980s, in both central and local government, the emphasis on a management approach based on the need for economy, efficiency and effectiveness has been reflected in new financial management systems and organizational structures (Henkel, 1991). The guides to appraisal published by the Treasury and other departments stress the importance of defining the objectives of a programme or project and relating them to underlying policies, but this may be particularly difficult in the public policy area where overall goals and priorities are not clear or are contradictory (Pollitt and Harrison, 1992). It may be that the more recent support for objectives-led assessment (SACTRA, 1992; Goodwin, 1991) represents a move away from conventional (and often flawed) cost-effectiveness or value-for-money studies.

A further complicating factor in the development of policy appraisal in the 1980s was the challenge to the assumption that the proper object of policy appraisal was government activity. This concept has itself been increasingly challenged during the decade with the 'rolling back of the state', and the emphasis on deregulation, such as in the White Papers *Lifting the Burden*, or *Building Businesses, not Barriers* (Her Majesty's Government, 1985). The UK government intended to minimize State intervention in favour of a framework-setting role for government, thereby enabling greater scope for private sector activity and initiative. It also adopted a policy of privatizing many of the government's assets, such as the former nationalized industries of gas, water and electricity, to increase efficiency, introduce competition, and to some extent to raise capital.

The case study of the UK energy sector, described in Chapter 5, illustrates many of the difficulties in undertaking an assessment of public policy when the government ostensibly intends only to establish a framework for the operation of the energy market.

2.5 Problems with strategic environmental assessment

The application of EIA at a strategic level is therefore likely to be subject to many of the difficulties encountered in conventional policy analysis, as well as the problems already encountered in the EIA of projects.

In summary, these problems include:

- the often nebulous nature of proposals at the level of policies and plans, and the tendency for decisions regarding PPPs to be made in an incremental and not clearly formulated fashion;

- the problems of system boundaries: the large number of potential decisions that flow from a higher-level decision, and the large number of potential developments over a physical or policy area, and thus the consequent analytical complexity required;

- lack of information about existing and projected future environmental conditions; lack of information about the nature, scale and location of future development proposals; and thus the lack of precision with which these impacts can be predicted;

- the large number and variety of alternatives to be considered at the different stages of policy formulation;

- lack of shared information about the experience of EIA at the strategic level, and a dearth of cases in which it has been applied, especially to policies (this book is one contribution to reducing this problem);

- the uncertainty over public involvement in the policy-making process;

- the political nature of the decision-making process.

These problems will be addressed in greater detail in the following chapters. But, notwithstanding these difficulties, SEA is justified in terms of allowing a more explicit trade-off to be made between objectives, and of enabling a more consistent integration of environmental concerns into decision-making. It may be that different forms of SEA are appropriate for different levels of decision-making, with their own distinct characteristics. This too is considered in subsequent chapters.

3:

Existing and proposed systems of strategic environmental assessment

This chapter reviews some of the SEA systems (or near equivalents) currently in existence or recently proposed. It shows the variety of procedural and methodological approaches taken to SEA to date, and gives an indication of the feasibility of conducting SEAs on a broader scale. The SEA systems of California and the Netherlands provide particularly good examples: California's system has been in operation for 20 years, and has resulted in the carrying out of hundreds of SEAs, and the Dutch government is developing an ambitious expanded SEA system based on the principle of sustainable development. The chapter concludes with an overview of the various systems of SEA, to identify trends and to emphasize their similarities and differences.

3.1 United States

National system

The regulatory basis for SEA, like that of project EIA, began with the US National Environmental Policy Act of 1969 (NEPA). NEPA sets out a national environmental policy and, as a means of achieving this policy, requires that all federal agencies prepare a 'detailed statement' on the environmental impacts of 'every recommendation or report on proposals for legislation and other major federal actions significantly affecting the quality of the human environment' (US Govt., 1970). Over the years, the procedural details of preparing these statements have attracted much more attention than the NEPA's other provisions, and the EIA process has focused primarily on individual projects rather than on PPPs.

However, attention has recently begun to shift towards the more neglected aspects of the NEPA, and the US is showing a revived interest in SEA-related topics. A series of court cases of 1988-91 concerning the need and scope for cumulative impact analysis seem to be going beyond the narrow rulings of the late 1970s and into a new era in which such issues as global warming, loss of species diversity and ozone depletion are gaining in importance (Herson and Bogdan, 1991). Whereas an influential early court ruling (Kleppe v. Sierra Club, 427 US 390, 1976) held that a cumulative impact analysis was needed only for formally proposed actions, not more informal 'programs', more recent rulings[1] have rejected NEPA documents on the grounds of inadequate cumulative impact analysis. Agencies seem to be particularly vulnerable to these challenges if they appear to be acting in bad faith by segmenting larger projects or ignoring closely connected projects.

The Council on Environmental Quality guidelines of 1978, which interpret the requirements of the NEPA, note that EIA may be necessary for the following actions:

1. Adoption of official policy, such as rules, regulations and interpretations.
2. Adoption of formal plans, such as official documents... which guide or prescribe alternative uses of federal resources.
3. Adoption of programs, such as a group of concerted actions to implement a specific policy or plan.
4. Approval of specific projects. (USCEQ, 1978).

They also note that, when preparing an EIA, agencies should evaluate the proposals:

1. Geographically, including actions occurring in the same general location, such as body of water, region, or metropolitan area.
2. Generically, including actions that have relevant similarities, such as common timing, impacts, alternatives, methods of implementation, media, or subject matter.
3. By stage of technological development. (USCEQ, 1978).

The guidelines recommend that an EIA should include a cover sheet, summary and table of contents; a discussion of the purpose of and need for the action and alternatives; a discussion of the affected environment, and of the environmental consequences of the action and alternatives; a list of preparers and of organizations to whom copies of the statement are sent; and an index (USCEQ, 1978).

In response to the NEPA's requirements, most federal agencies have established separate regulations that incorporate EIA into their various programmes (eg. US Dept. of Energy, 1992a; US Dept. of the Interior, 1980). Agencies are encouraged to prepare broad EISs that cover policies or programmes, and to use a form of tiering when addressing subsequent projects within the policy or programme. These federal agency regulations often cover specific kinds of projects, anticipated impacts, and/or sensitive areas (UNECE, 1991a). EIA is also integrated into the legislative process of Congress.

One source notes that approximately 320 'programmatic environmental impact statements' (PEISs) were prepared between 1979 and 1989, primarily by the Environmental Protection Agency (Sigal and Webb, 1989). However, a more recent document by the Forest Service shows that 470 PEISs were prepared by that agency alone between 1970 and 1992 (Ketcham, 1992). Examples of federal-level PEISs include those for:

Box 3.1 **SEA for restructuring the US nuclear weapons complex**
(US Dept. of Energy, 1992b)

The Nuclear Weapons Complex (NWC) is a set of interrelated facilities that design, manufacture, test, maintain, and ultimately dismantle nuclear weapons in the US. The NWC consists of 12 sites, which can be broadly split into three functional elements: nuclear materials recycling and manufacturing, non-nuclear manufacturing, and research and development. Much of the NWC is more than 30 years old, and in need of major repairs or modernization. The recent reduction in nuclear weapons requirements also means that the NWC offers more capacity than necessary. The US Department of Energy proposes to restructure the NWC to make it smaller, less diverse, and less expensive to operate.

In February 1992, the Department of Energy produced an implementation plan that provides guidance for the preparation of a Programmatic Environmental Impact Statement (PEIS) for this restructuring. After a period of public consultation regarding the scope of the PEIS, a draft PEIS is expected (at the time of writing) to be published in December 1992. A final PEIS is expected in July 1993 after further public consultation.

The PEIS is likely to consider two options. The first option would relocate and/or eliminate activities at one of the 12 NWC sites, along with necessary upgrading at the other sites. The second option would involve amalgamating and relocating two or more of the NWC sites. The PEIS will also analyse the impacts of providing a new tritium supply capacity; this had already been addressed in a separate draft EIS, but will be reassessed as part of the new PEIS. In the longer term, project-specific EIAs will be prepared; these will be based on the PEIS, simplifying the analysis needed.

The PEIS is expected to consider the environmental consequences of constructing and operating support facilities, transporting complex materials, and both normal and accidental radiological and non-radiological releases. Impacts to be considered include those on public and worker health and safety, air quality, water resources, biological resources, cultural and palaeontological resources, transportation, socioeconomic conditions, and other issues identified through the scoping exercise.

- noxious weed control programmes at various national forests (Ketcham, 1992);

- a management plan for the Boundary Waters Canoe Area (Ketcham, 1992);

- the Coal Technology Demonstration Program (US Dept. of Energy, 1989);

- a programme for installing and operating Terminal Doppler Weather Radars at airports across the US (US Dept. of Transport, 1991);

- a programme for the disposal of chemical stockpiles (Wagner, 1991a);

- a programme for restructuring the nuclear arms complex (US Dept. of Energy, 1992b) (see Box 3.1).

Of these, the procedures of the US Department of Housing and Urban Development are the most comprehensive; they are discussed below.

In addition, 28 of the 50 states of the US have instituted some form of additional EIA procedures through state regulations. Some of these systems encourage the preparation of EIAs for PPPs, but they mostly limit EIA to projects. California has by far the most comprehensive and effective state SEA system; this is discussed below.

US Department of Housing and Urban Development (HUD)

The HUD prepared an 'Areawide Environmental Impact Assessment Guidebook' in 1981 that was designed to assist in assessing the impacts of alternative patterns of urban development or redevelopment in metropolitan-scale areas. This guide presents a detailed methodology for assessing these impacts, which is summarized in Table 3.1. The methodology is broadly similar to that for preparing project EIAs, but adds three preliminary steps: determination of need, establishment of the area and data to be analysed, and identification of alternatives.

The guidebook proposes that an areawide EIA should consider 21 topics, namely land development suitability, volcanic and tectonic activity, agricultural lands, unique natural features, water supply, water quality, significant habitats and species, flooding, climatic hazards, fire hazards, air quality, noise, energy, hazardous materials, solid waste, community services, employment opportunities, social conditions, visual quality, historic resources, and archaeological resources. For each of these topics, the guidebook provides guidance on techniques under the following headings:

- — *issues:* impacts and concerns at the areawide scale;
- — *assessment questions:* purpose of the areawide study;
- — *base data:* data requirements for assessing impacts;
- — *impact assessment techniques:* specific procedures, calculations, models, mapping tasks, etc. to estimate environmental impacts;
- — *evaluation:* explanation of procedures for comparing impact predictions with existing regulations and other standards;
- — *mitigation measures:* description of the most cost-effective techniques for minimizing predicted adverse impacts;
- — *references:* key sources.

Table 3.1 **US Department of Housing and Urban Development methodology for areawide EIA**
(US Dept. of HUD, 1981)

1. **Determine need/feasibility:**
   indicators of need;
   availability of data, expertise, funds;
   prepare study design.

2. **Establish area boundaries, analysis units, environmental data base:**
   availability of data;
   location of expected change;
   location of resources/hazards;
   jurisdictional boundaries;
   compatibility with anticipated impact issues.

3. **Identify areawide alternatives:**
   research local and areawide plans, programmes, etc.;
   define areawide alternatives: totals, 'theme', etc.;
   Allocate areawide totals to analysis units:
   by land use type, resource type, etc.

4. **Scoping:**
   identify key issues;
   eliminate nonpertinent issues;
   establish work plan: revise/finalize area boundaries, data collection plan, report format.

5. **Environmental analysis:**
   document baseline conditions (analysis unit scale): presence or absence, quantity, sensitivity/significance, trends, past changes if significant;
   establish units or multipliers of demand and/or consumption (per capita, per household, by industry, etc.);
   estimate impacts: for each environmental component and for each alternative begin at analysis unit scale, aggregate for area scale.

6. **Impact synthesis and evaluation:**
   identify evaluation standards/criteria/preferences;
   evaluate impacts for each environmental component;
   compare alternatives.

7. **Recommendations:**
   identify mitigation measures (prevention, compensation, substitution);
   identify preferred alternative (if possible).

The HUD describes the major advantages of SEA, in terms that still hold good:

> The areawide approach is particularly well suited to environmental assessment in areas expecting new or renewed urban development. Cumulative effects of projected development can be identified as can appropriate mitigation measures... At the time specific individual projects are proposed, those projects can be evaluated within the pre-established context of the area wide assessment... This approach assures that likely project impacts are evaluated on a more comprehensive, cumulative, areawide basis. It also increases the usefulness of the analysis because decisionmakers can eventually become more and more familiar with the data and context of each environmental impact statement for that area (US Dept. of HUD, 1981).

More than ten years after its publication, the guidebook still provides one of the most comprehensive formal methodologies for SEA.

California

The state government of California requires the preparation of SEAs through the California Environmental Quality Act (CEQA) (State of California, 1986). This act, as implemented by the State CEQA Guidelines, requires EIAs to be conducted for PPPs as well as for individual projects. More than 130 'programmatic environmental impact reports' (PEIRs) are prepared annually in California (Bass, 1990). California's SEA system is likely to be the most developed and operational system in the world.

The CEQA requires public agencies to prepare SEAs for series of linked actions, including projects that are related:

1. geographically;
2. as logical parts in the chain of contemplated actions;
3. in connection with issuance of rules, regulations, plans... or
4. as individual activities carried out under the same authorizing statutory or regulatory authority and having generally similar environmental effects which can be mitigated in similar ways (State of California, 1986).

Of the 342 SEAs received by California's State Clearinghouse between January 1988 and July 1990, 33 per cent were city and county plans, 31 per cent were specific plans, 10 per cent were community plans, and 7 per cent were development plans. Other SEAs concerned water management programmes, parks and recreation plans, airport master plans, university master plans, transportation plans, air quality regulations, conservation programmes, hazardous waste management plans, and growth management plans (Bass, 1990). Examples of these PEISs include analyses of:

- a general plan update for the town of Tiburon;

- a plan for water reclamation and re-use for the city of San Diego;

- a plan for the Jack London State Historic Park;

- an airport plan for Auburn City;

- a hazardous waste management plan for Los Angeles County;

- a regional transport plan for San Diego (Bass, 1990) and

- a comprehensive plan for San Joaquin County (see Box 3.2).

County and city authorities are encouraged to combine the processes of comprehensive planning and SEA as long as they satisfy the requirements of both the state planning law and the CEQA.

The CEQA's requirements concerning the content of the SEA are again similar to those required for a project EIA, namely:

- a table of contents;

- a brief summary of the proposed action and its impacts;

- a description of the action which includes its location, statement of objectives, description of its technical, economic and environmental characteristics, and a listing of the agencies expected to use the document in their decision making;

- an 'environmental setting' section that includes local and regional information and a discussion of any relevant adopted plans and policies affected by the proposed action;

- an evaluation of the action's impacts, including direct, indirect, long-term, short-term, unavoidable, cumulative and growth-inducing effects;

- alternatives to the proposed action, including alternative sites, which would reduce or avoid the significant impacts;

- a statement briefly indicating the reasons why some possible environmental impacts were determined not to be significant and were, therefore, not evaluated;

- a list of all organizations consulted during preparation of the report;

- a list of all persons and organizations commenting on the report;

- the responses of the public agency to those comments (State of California, 1986).

***Box 3.2* SEA for the San Joaquin County Comprehensive Planning Program**

(Baseline Environmental Consulting, 1991)

San Joaquin County covers approximately 373,600 ha in central California. The county's Community Development Department produced a Comprehensive Planning Program (CPP) in 1991, which consisted of a three-volume county general plan, a general plan map, and a 'county development title', which includes zoning maps. This CPP was subject to an environmental impact report (EIR) that was required prior to adoption of the program. The CPP forecasts an 80 per cent population growth and 64 per cent employment growth for San Joaquin County between 1990 and 2010. It identifies areas for new residential, commercial and industrial development in existing urban communities to accommodate 70 per cent of this growth, and sites for five new/expanded communities to accommodate the remaining 30 per cent of the growth.

A draft EIR (DEIR) was prepared for this CPP by Baseline Environmental Consulting in December 1991. The DEIR considers 20 types of environmental impacts, including land use, water quality, library facilities, energy, and public health and safety. For each impact, it describes existing conditions under a 'setting' section, and the impacts of the CPP and possible mitigation measures in an 'impacts and mitigation measures' section. The focus of the impact analyses for the DEIR is on cumulative, countywide impacts. A variety of mitigation measures were proposed to reduce significant impacts to a level where they are no longer significant; these include changes to policies in the county general plan, to (enforceable) regulations in the county development title, and to various zoning maps.

The DEIR also considers alternatives to the CPP. These include concentrating all the population growth on the fringes of existing urban communities; not building/expanding the five new communities; reducing the area of new/expanded communities; and reducing the five new/expanded communities down to two.

The DEIR found that the amount of land designated for development by the CPP was 121 per cent more than would be needed to accommodate the projected population and employment growth. For this reason, the EIR recommended that the county seriously consider not approving the five new/expanded communities. In late July 1992, the County Board of Supervisors adopted the CPP and included only two of the five new/expanded communities.

Once an SEA has been prepared, specific projects that come under the scope of the PPP can be assessed. For each project, an initial study is conducted to determine whether the environmental impacts of the project were adequately addressed in the SEA. Those aspects addressed in the SEA need not be re-addressed in the project EIA; if enough aspects are addressed in the

SEA, no EIA for the project may be required. Many public agencies have used this principle of 'tiering' to save some of the cost and time involved in preparing multiple project EIAs.

The State CEQA Guidelines cite five advantages to preparing SEAs. The SEA can:

1. provide an occasion for a more exhaustive consideration of impacts and alternatives than would be practical in an EIA on an individual action;
2. ensure consideration of cumulative impacts that might be slighted in a case-by-case analysis;
3. avoid duplicative reconsideration of basic policy considerations;
4. allow the Lead Agency to consider broad policy alternatives and programwide mitigation measures at an early time when the agency has greater flexibility to deal with basic problems or cumulative impacts;
5. allow reduction in paperwork (State of California, 1986).

3.2 European Community

The EC has pursued an active environmental policy ever since it adopted its First Action Programme on the Environment in 1973. It began to commission research on EIA in 1975, and drew up a preliminary draft directive on EIA in 1978. Originally it was intended that this system should apply to plans as well as projects (Wood, 1988); however, by the time that EC Directive 85/337 was approved in June 1985, its application had been restricted to two lists of projects, as shown in Appendix A.1. Several member states have subsequently interpreted the directive to cover certain PPPs; these will be discussed in later sections.

Table 3.2 summarizes the status of SEA in various EC member states (CEC, 1991a). It also gives a summary of the member states' views of circumstances in which EIA may be beneficial at stages earlier than the project stage, as given in the EC's five-year review of the existing system of project EIA (CEC, 1991b). Table 3.2 shows a wide diversity of existing SEA systems in the EC, from the Netherlands' mandatory formal system, through various forms of less thorough and less official environmental evaluation, to no assessment of the environmental impacts of PPPs at all. Interestingly, some countries with minimal SEA systems, particularly Portugal, are quite enthusiastic about the potential application of SEA. In contrast Germany, which is already implementing a form of informal SEA, is much more cautious about its potential. In the meantime, the EC's work on SEA has continued. The EC's Fourth Action Programme on the Environment, agreed in 1987, stated:

> The Commission's concern will also be extended, as rapidly as possible, to cover policies and policy statements, plans and their implementation, procedures, programmes... as well as individual projects... the Commission is already working

on the development of effective internal procedures to ensure that environmental requirements are built into the processes of assessing and approving proposals for all developments to be financed from [Community] Funds... Once these procedures have been established... the Commission will consider the question of their wider application.... (CEC, 1987).

Similarly, the Fifth Action Programme on the Environment, agreed in 1992, which focuses on the need to achieve sustainable development, states:

> Given the goal of achieving sustainable development it seems only logical, if not essential, to apply an assessment of the environmental implications of all relevant policies, plans and programmes... An assessment of the implications for the environment will be made in the course of drawing up Community policies and legislation with special care taken in the areas on internal markets, internal trade, industry, energy, agriculture, transport, regional development and tourism; Member States should undertake similar integration by applying environmental impact assessment to their own plans and programmes (EC, 1992).

The Community's report to UNCED elaborates further on the justification for SEA, using examples of road project EIA that does not consider alternative options such as rail, and the incremental effects of small-scale irrigation schemes on steppe habitats (CEC, 1991c).

The EC's experience of providing grants for investments in the poorer parts of the Community under the EC Structural Funds has confirmed the need for SEA. The requirement more recently has been for countries to apply for Structural Fund assistance through 'Operational Programmes', multi-annual investment plans that are much less able to specify the types and locations of specific development projects. In some cases these projects have been environmentally harmful and in conflict with EC goals, yet under the existing project-based directive the EC can only require that EIA be carried out on the projects, not on the whole programme. By the time the project assessment is complete, it is often too late to alter substantially the proposals for which Structural Fund money is allocated (Montgomery, 1990).

The Commission's experience of the difficulty of assessing the environmental impact of Structural Fund operations under a programme-based system may be leading it to introduce a form of SEA independently of the proposed directive. At the time of writing the Commission is reviewing the Structural Fund Regulations. It is believed that consideration is being given to introducing a system of 'environmental profiles', whereby member states would be required to provide a range of information on the environment in the region concerned in conjunction with applications for Structural Fund assistance. The Commission apparently recognizes that much of this data will not currently be available, and is prepared to provide financial assistance for its collection. Doubts still persist as to the use of this information in decisions on the funding of development schemes (i.e. whether funds will be conditional on satisfactory environmental information being provided).

The Community's recent Directive 92/43 on the Conservation of Natural Habitats and of Wild Fauna and Flora makes a passing reference to the principle of SEA in laying down tests that must be met before any development is permitted that may have significant effects on a so-called Special Area of Conservation or SAC. Article 6(3) states:

> Any *plan* or project not directly connected with or necessary to the management of the [SAC] but likely to have a significant effect thereon, *either individually or in combination with other plans or projects*, shall be subject to appropriate assessment of its implications for the site in view of the site's conservation objectives (emphasis added).

Table 3.2 **Current SEA systems and views on potential SEA systems in EC member states**
(CEC 1991a, CEC 1991b)
note: EE = environmental evaluation, which is less stringent than SEA.

Country	Present system of SEA	Member states' views on circumstances where pre-project assessment may be beneficial
Belgium	n/a	There is a clear need for EIA at a higher, more strategic planning level. A two-stage approach, with a broader more strategic study early in the process, and a more selectively focused study for individual projects later would be appropriate. Infrastructure developments particularly suffer from EE starting too late in the planning process.
Denmark	n/a	Action plans on development and the environment issued by the Danish government, e.g. 'Action Plan against Pollution of the Danish Marine Environment by Nutrients' (1987) should include an EIA.
France	SEA has been undertaken for some forms of land use plans, and EE for others. The findings of these studies are incorporated into the PPP report.	There is a growing acknowledgement that EIA should be extended to programmes and plans, at least initially in relation to linear infrastructure projects. Some research has been undertaken on this aspect in France.

Germany	Most PPPs with environmental implications are subject to informal EE. The findings of these studies are generally incorporated into the PPP report. Most plans are reviewed by an independent environmental authority.	EIA should be considered for PPPs that lead to certain projects, particularly where alternative locations need to be considered. EIA for PPPs should be developed carefully and accompanied by good case studies and pilot projects.
Greece	EEs are generally required only for resource and waste management plans. These EE findings are dispersed throughout the PPP report.	n/a
Ireland	n/a	EIA at PPP level would complement project EIA
Italy	EE is conducted for some state sectors (e.g. energy, mining) and for most regional land use plans. The EE findings are contained in the planning document. A draft law has been proposed for application of SEA to land use programmes.	There is support for introducing EIA at earlier stages, e.g. at plan and programme level, but this should not lead to any reduction in projects covered by EIA.
Luxembourg	n/a	It would be useful if the EIA of new industries took place at the level of regional plans for the determination of industrial areas. Project level EIA would then not need to analyse aspects already dealt with at this preceding stage.
Netherlands	Formal EIA has been required since 1987 for sectoral plans on waste management, drinking water supply, energy and electricity supply and some land use plans. The EE findings are reported in a separate document.	EIA is mandatory in the Netherlands for certain aspects of policy plans, such as choice of sites, determination of road/railway routes, etc. The information gained from EIA at such levels is useful for decisions by central government.
Portugal	Some partial EE of PPPs has taken place, but SEA is not a normal procedure.	EIA of PPPs would be a useful planning tool in providing an insight to real alternatives, the clear identification of significant impacts, and in the assessment of cumulative and synergistic effects.

Spain	Some PPPs have been subject to EE, for instance those for waste management, water and infrastructure provision. The findings of the EE are normally incorporated into the PPP document as a separate chapter.	The assessment of many developments could be better handled at stages other than project level, mainly those where location is the key point, such as linear infrastructure, energy plants, and activities that affect a broad area.
UK	Most PPPs with environmental implications contain some form of EE. The findings of the EE are incorporated into the PPP document.	Linear and other types of developments might be better dealt with at a more strategic level, in the first instance at the PPP level, before being dealt with in a more specific and detailed way.

The European Commission's Directorate-General XI (DG XI) has proposed a directive on SEA, which was released to national experts in March 1991, but has not yet been approved. The proposed directive is reportedly being opposed by a number of the 'larger' member states. It has been substantially altered by DG XI but the new version has not yet been released (Therivel et al., 1992). The Fifth Action Programme on the Environment sets the target date for application of SEA at 1995 and beyond; this is probably a realistic target. The remainder of this section discusses the first version of the proposed directive.

The proposed directive identifies three bodies who would be involved in preparing and reviewing SEAs. The 'lead authority' would be the one preparing the PPP, and would also undertake the SEA. The 'competent authority' would take account of the SEA before approving the PPP. Finally, the 'designated environmental authority' would review the adequacy of the SEA, the likely environmental impacts, and mitigation measures; may advise on the scope of the SEA; and would give an opinion to the competent authority if the lead authority applied for an exemption to the SEA process.

SEAs would apply to sectoral, regional and other PPPs. Sectoral SEAs would be required for PPPs relating to agriculture, forestry or fishing, energy, extraction and processing of minerals, water supply, transport, tourism and waste disposal. Regional SEAs would be required for PPPs relating to land use and development, including urban land use plans, and particularly to urban reconstruction or the growth of urban areas. Member states could also require SEAs for PPPs relating to the future development and operation of activities in other sectors; to PPPs not directly implemented through projects, such as research and development and fiscal policies; and to revisions of PPPs. Member states could allow individual PPPs to be exempt from assessment, either because they would not give rise to significant environmental impacts or because their significant impacts were assessed at other stages in the planning process.

The contents of the SEA would include a discussion of the following:

- the PPP and its main objectives;

- how environmental effects were taken into account when formulating its objectives and content;

- aspects of the environment and of the area likely to be affected;

- likely significant effects on the environment of the PPP and main alternatives; reasons for choosing the proposed action;

- mitigation measures proposed and adopted for the proposed action, including EA at subsequent stages;

- compatibility of the proposed action with relevant environmental legislation (EC or national);

- monitoring arrangements;

- an outline of difficulties encountered in compiling information;

- a non-technical summary.

Impacts on human beings, fauna, flora, landscape, natural resources, cultural heritage, and material assets would need to be considered for the favoured option and its main alternatives. The compatibility of the PPP with the objectives of environmental protection established at the EC and national level for the sector concerned, and the consistency of the PPP with actions taken at an EC or national level to achieve these objectives, would also need to be considered. Appendix B.1 summarizes the main benefits and limitations of the proposed directive.

At the time of writing (mid-1992), the UK government's official stance on the proposed directive on SEA was that it was not yet developed enough: that it is being developed too quickly, and that too many issues still need to be considered and worked out. In a Parliamentary answer of May 1991, David Trippier, the then Environment Minister, stated:

> I could not possibly put my weight behind the proposals as currently constituted by the Commission because they are, in truth, half-baked... The proposals suggested by the European Commission are in a mess and the vast majority of the member states accept that. I hope that they will be tidied up so that we can achieve our objectives.... (House of Commons Official Report, 8 May 1991).

In October 1991, David Trippier expanded on these views:

> We fully agree with the purpose of the proposal – to ensure that environmental considerations are properly taken into account in public decision-making... The UK's doubts about the Commission's proposals do not arise because we cannot

live with the basic idea. Our doubts are occasioned by the form of the proposal. It would require, by law, that certain procedures be applied to all decisions on policies, plans and programmes. But such decisions are not arrived at by going through certain procedural hoops to which you can add an environmental stage. Policy is developing all the time – it involves repeated toing and froing between the many people involved... there is often no single moment when a decision is made.

The problem with the Commission proposal is that it either requires formal EIA at all these stages, or it leaves it extremely uncertain when EIA is required. Obviously different governments will face these problems to different degrees, but all democratic governments will have them.

In our view the principle of subsidiarity applies: decisions of this kind are properly for national governments to make (DoE, 1991b).

The UK government gives three major arguments against a formal system of SEA (Braun, 1992). First, as was discussed in Chapter 2, for most PPPs there does not exist a clear moment in time when a decision is made. For most projects, the decision comes when the local planning authority decides whether or not to give planning permission. For PPPs, however, the types of decisions vary greatly in terms of formality, levels of government concerned, types of procedures involved, levels of consultation, spending plans involved, and type of government structure. Often these decisions are not one-off decisions but involve a process of negotiation. Different organizations may make different announcements on the same decision. Thus any SEA procedures would have to be extremely flexible to accommodate the large variety of types of decision and the inherent uncertainty of some decisions.

Second, SEA would require expertise that agencies currently do not have. It would require agencies to determine the level of existing environmental resources and their carrying capacities, plan for the future using these environmental resources as a measuring stick, and periodically revise its SEA. This procedure involves expertise that is not inherent to the agencies concerned; it involves a large number of highly-trained experts, and considerable further development of environmental valuation techniques.

Finally, SEA would involve the need for agencies to go to outside sources for environmental information, and for agreement with SEA-related decisions. It is likely that SEA would require the establishment of an environmental agency, which would coordinate environmental information to avoid duplication and differences in interpretation between agencies, determine environmental carrying capacities, and advise other agencies on SEA techniques and related decisions. In particular, the proposed EC directive presupposes some form of independent environmental agency; the government has already stated its opposition to the formation of such an agency.

The proposed directive on SEA draws heavily on Directive 85/337 on EIA of projects. This has several advantages. Negotiations concerning such issues as what impacts need to be addressed in an SEA could be shortened, since they will already have been agreed in the context of Directive 85/337. The SEA system would benefit from the experience accrued in implementing the provisions of Directive 85/337; in turn this could make the implementation of SEA less disruptive and less costly. Finally, some of the institutional frameworks that needed to be set up for Directive 85/337 (e.g. library of EISs, training of assessors) could be used directly or modified only slightly for the process of SEA, saving time and money; it must be noted that not all of these matters are completely operational yet.

However, the proposal also has disadvantages. First, any limitations of Directive 85/337 could be carried over to the SEA directive. An example of this is the dual listing of which PPPs require SEA, where SEA is mandatory for some PPPs but only discretionary for others. Another example is the incomplete list of potential environmental impacts. Second, DG XI may not give adequate consideration to procedures or techniques which are not required by Directive 85/337 but which could improve the SEA directive. Examples include the establishment of a framework for decision-making using the results of SEA; consideration of issues such as risk and equity in SEA; and, significantly, the use of the sustainability concept as a cornerstone for SEA. Finally, the true implications of implementing SEA may not be considered. The proposed directive's statement that the 'scale of assessment activities involved in respect of PPPs is likely to be significantly less than that required for projects' seems to underestimate the work involved in SEA.

3.3 Netherlands

SEA has been formally required in the Netherlands since 1987 for sectoral plans on waste management, drinking water supply, energy and electricity supply, and for some land use plans. The findings of these SEAs are reviewed by a special commission, and are generally subject to public consultation. A study carried out in 1990 by the Netherlands Commission for Environmental Impact Assessment provided an early indication of the success and failure of the country's SEA system to date. The study showed that a number of provincial waste management plans and provincial mineral extraction plans had been subject to SEA. These SEAs ranged from documents that provided a basis for concrete decisions to those that established only general strategic directions for action, with the latter predominating. The SEAs tended to be very comprehensive, often with much information that did not pertain to decision-making or made the documents too complex. These early SEAs were felt to have little influence on decision-making; a main reason for this appeared to be that the SEAs were drawn up only after a decision on the plan had already been taken. Many of the resulting plans 'failed to reach decisions other than long-term resolves' (Huisman, 1990).

As discussed in Chapter 1, changes to this SEA system are currently being made that will substantially broaden its field of application and that will relate it more closely to the principle of sustainable development. The National Environmental Policy Plan of 1989 contains two main SEA-related actions. The first (Action A141) requires existing policy areas to be assessed to determine how well they fulfil the objective of sustainable development:

> The government will give an account of how the recommendations contained in the Brundtland Report are to be given substance in each ministry and area of policy. At the same time there will also be an assessment of the extent to which the instruments of the various policy areas contribute to effecting sustainable development. Exploratory work will, in any case, be carried out in the following areas of policy: physical planning policy, housing, technology, markets and prices, energy, science, traffic, fiscal policy, agriculture, justice/enforcement, education, industry (Govt. of the Netherlands, 1989b).

To implement this requirement, the government is establishing a methodology to determine a given policy's relevance to, and ability to contribute to the fulfilment of, sustainable development. This proposed methodology consists of a checklist for environmental aspects that may be considered with respect to sustainability, and a list of questions to be answered. The methodology is likely to take the form of a short (3 to 4 page), non-mandatory document, as shown in Table 3.3 (van der Lee, 1992).

The second action (Action A142) requires that, 'for policy proposals which might have important consequences for the environment, information on these effects will be provided' (Govt. of the Netherlands, 1989b). The implementation of this requirement is partially under way, as a 'section on the environment' must already be prepared for plans for civil aviation sites, drinking and industrial water supply, power supply, waste disposal and excavation, as well as for rural plans, some regional plans, and key national planning decisions establishing outline choices of location. This 'section on the environment' is a written presentation of the repercussions of the action on the environment.

However, the Evaluation Commission on the Environmental Protection Act has recommended that these procedures be expanded to make the preparation of a 'section on the environment' mandatory for all policy plans with repercussions for the environment. The exact contents of this 'section on the environment' have not yet been finalized, and the government is still working on preparing relevant guidelines:

> The introduction of a section on the environment raises various questions... For the time being the government will confine itself to identifying the most important questions, designating a number of starting points and indicating the route along which work will continue.
>
> Before the introduction [of such a section], the following questions must be examined:

Table 3.3 Dutch methodology for screening existing government policy areas
(van der Lee, 1992)

Checklist for sustainable development:

- energy consumption (eg. natural gas, oil, coal);

- quality of applied production processes and technologies;

- quality of products;

- use of renewable natural resources and raw materials (eg. timber, fish);

- quantity and quality of waste flows and emissions to air, soil and water;

- use of open space; impact on [their] existing function;

- use of non-renewable natural resources and raw materials (eg. sand, clay, marl, ground-water and spring-water).

Questions to be answered:

- Have environmental policy goals been taken into account in the planning and decision-making process on the instrument?

- To what extent can environmental interests and sustainable development be taken into account in the implementation of the policy?

- Does the instrument contribute to a greater knowledge of the environmental consequences of the policy and enlarge the support of target groups in society for sustainable development?

- What are the intended and the unintended (side-) effects of the deployment of the policy instrument on activities and behaviour of society?

- Do the intended effects lead to the re-use of raw materials, waste prevention and recycling, restriction of mobility (car, train, aeroplane), energy savings, the use of sustainable energy and the like?

- What are the consequences of the unintended side-effects of the policy instrument on sustainable development?

- Do instruments of other policy areas contribute to these side-effects?

- To what extent do the effects of the instrument contribute to or hamper sustainable development?

- field of application;

- cases for which the [EIA] must be applied (in other words, which policy plans have repercussions for the environment); the [EIA] is not a replacement for the mandatory [project] EIA, but is intended for policy plans not [previously] requiring EIA;

- it is not necessary or possible to give identical information for all policy plans; the extent and depth of information on repercussions for the environment is influenced by the interest of the environment and how radical the policy plan in question is;

- responsibility: the department initiating the policy should be responsible for drafting the section on the environment at national level; the Minister of Housing, Physical Planning and Environment in his role as coordinating Minister for the Environment could be responsible for monitoring the quality of the section on the environment, for example through the possibility of making comments or additions to it;

- procedural aspects [eg. institutional cooperation]....

The government is aiming at a practical and pragmatic approach to [EIA].... (van der Lee, 1992).

The final form of the Dutch SEA system, and its effectiveness when implemented, is certain to be of great interest to other countries considering establishing sustainability-based SEA systems.

3.4 United Kingdom

The UK has no formal procedure for SEA. The Department of the Environment's guide *Policy Appraisal and the Environment* and its Planning Policy Guidance Note 12 (PPG12) are the UK's closest equivalent to a formal system of SEA; these are discussed below. However, a number of one-off or partial SEAs have been prepared in the UK either in response to local authority pressure or as a systematic method of fulfilling the requirements of other (pollution-control) legislation. Examples include:

- a 1992 study for three water authorities to determine the best way of meeting the demand for water in Kent over the next 30 years (Binnie & Partners, 1991) (see Box 3.3);

- a 1988 study by North West Water to determine what works were needed to achieve the EC bathing water standards along a defined length of the Fylde Coast (North West Water, 1988);

- a 1988 SEA by Thames Water Authority covering 60 projects related to the Lower Colne Flood Defence Scheme (discussed in CPRE, 1991);

- a study in the mid-1980s by Cheshire County Council which attempted to assess the impacts of possible industrial expansion on two large (250 ha) sites near an existing petrochemical complex in the Mersey Marshes area (Wood, 1988).

Box 3.3 SEA for water provision in Kent (UK)
(Binnie & Partners, 1991)

Water demand in Kent is likely to rise over the next 30 years. Recognizing this future demand, three water companies – Mid Kent Water plc, Southern Water Services Ltd, and Dover Water Services Ltd – formed a joint steering committee to consider ways of dealing with this demand. They appointed a firm of consulting engineers, Binnie & Partners, and an environmental consultancy, Oakwood Environmental, to carry out an EIA on various options for dealing with the projected demand. The aims of the study were to demonstrate and quantify demand for additional water resources, undertake a phased programme of public consultation, identify and examine different water supply options, quantify the costs and benefits of each viable option, select a preferred option and identify the environmental impacts of the preferred option.

The options identified in the first stage of the study of 1991 included water conservation (leakage reduction, water metering, drought restrictions etc.), construction of a surface reservoir, improved management of groundwater sources, re-use of effluent from sewage treatment works, desalinization of brackish groundwater, and bulk transfer via mains or existing waterways.

The consultants undertook an extensive consultation programme with both statutory and non-statutory organizations and individuals. Consultation took place when the major options to be assessed were determined, when the impacts of various options were identified, and after the choice of options was made, to identify matters requiring further study. Consultations are expected to continue when planning and licence applications for the new resource are submitted.

Policy Appraisal and the Environment

The government White Paper on the Environment of 1990, *This Common Inheritance*, stressed the importance of taking environmental considerations fully into account in policy development, and committed the government to publishing guidance on the topic:

> There is scope for a more systematic approach within Government to the appraisal of the environmental costs and benefits before decisions are taken. The Government has therefore set work in hand to produce guidelines for policy appraisal where there are significant implications for the environment... The aim is to provide general guidance to departments, not to set out a rigid set of procedures to be followed in all cases (SoS, 1990).

The resulting guide, *Policy Appraisal and the Environment*, was prepared by the Department of the Environment based on a consultants' report and supervised by a committee chaired by the Treasury. It was released on 23

September 1991, and copies were distributed to central government mid-level managers (Braun, 1992).

The first annual report on the White Paper, which was published by government shortly after *Policy Appraisal and the Environment*, indicated the ways in which the guide would be used:

This guide... will assist with the introduction of a commonly accepted and systematic approach to the treatment of environmental issues in policy making and analysis. The guide is primarily intended for use by Civil Service administrators but it will be useful in any part of the public service where there are policies which involve the allocation of resources. It may also be of use to the private sector. The Government will follow up the publication of this guide with training and further publicity and will review the operation of the guide once it has become established and consider whether further action is needed to ensure environmental issues remain at the forefront of decision making (SoS, 1991).

The goal of *Policy Appraisal and the Environment* is to promote a form of 'cultural change', a different and broader way of thinking for civil servants (Braun, 1992). It is not meant to be a forced procedure, nor a future regulation, but rather to assist civil servants to begin to consider the environmental repercussions of their decisions. To this end, it proposes a step-by-step procedure for assessing the environmental effects of policies, along with a variety of techniques for valuing the environment.

The guide applies to a broad range of PPPs, since it contends that:

most areas of domestic policy have some environmental impact... In general, any policy or programme which concerns changes in the use of land or resources, or which involves the production or use of materials or energy, will have some environmental impact.

As examples of applicable PPPs, the guide lists those pertaining to agriculture, industry, energy, transport, communications, defence, planning and housing policies. Although the guide is specifically addressed to policies and programmes, it notes that much of its advice is also applicable to projects. PPG12, the first document directly to recommend the use of the procedures listed in the guide, applies to local authority statutory development plans; it is thus likely that the guide will first be formally applied to plans and programmes, and only later to policies.

Under these guidelines, the department or agency from where the PPP originates is to carry out the policy appraisal. The guide gives no clear indication of the content expected in an SEA. However, it does give a clear procedure to follow, and from this the possible content of a policy appraisal can be predicted:

- summary of the policy issue;
- objectives of the policy;
- constraints on the policy;

- options to the policy, including the 'do-nothing' and 'do-minimum' options;

- costs and benefits of the policy, including environmental impacts;

- weighing up of the costs and benefits of the policy, concentrating on key issues;

- a sensitivity analysis of the options;

- the preferred option, including the main factors affecting the choice;

- procedures for monitoring (if necessary) and evaluation at a later stage.

The guide lists what it considers to be 'environmental receptors', namely air and atmosphere, water resources, water bodies (size and situation), soil, geology, landscape, climate, energy (light and other electromagnetic radiation; noise and vibration), human beings (physical and mental health and well-being), cultural heritage, and other living organisms (flora and fauna). It implies that this is a list of impacts to consider in policy appraisal, but does not definitely state this.

The guide presents a range of methods for weighing up, quantifying and comparing the costs and benefits of different policy options. It shows a strong emphasis on quantification, and particularly for monetary valuation. In this, it differs from other SEA systems considered: generally their emphasis is on procedure rather than methodology.

The guide gives no clear procedure for incorporating public opinions and concerns into policy appraisal. It mentions the need to take public views into consideration in policy-making, but notes that 'in practice pressures of time and problems of confidentiality may restrict the amount of consultation that can be undertaken'. There would be no external review of the SEA, and it would be prepared for internal consumption only.

Appendix B.2 examines further the main benefits and limitations of *Policy Appraisal and the Environment*. The means of implementing the procedures suggested in the guide have not been specified, but a number of training programmes are planned, as well as a programme to monitor the progress of policy appraisal (Braun, 1992). However interviews during the drafting of this book with two key government departments revealed that neither of them had made specific provisions for integration of the guide's procedures into departmental practices or procedures.

Although the publication of *Policy Appraisal and the Environment* was primarily intended for 'those in central government who are charged with advising ministers on policies', it was also considered to be useful for any public service involved in policies for resource allocation. It is therefore likely that, in the future, other documents will refer to it. One such reference is to be found in the Department of the Environment's Planning Policy Guidance note (PPG12) on Development Plans and Regional Planning Guidance (DoE, 1992e). The PPG series is prepared by the government, after public consultation, to explain statutory provisions and guidance on policies and the operation of the planning system to local authorities and others.

Planning Policy Guidance Note 12

PPG12 was issued in February 1992, following consideration of comments on the consultation draft of 1991. Its ostensible purpose is to explain the provisions of the Planning and Compensation Act 1991 as they relate to the status and coverage of development plans. The act also amends the Town and Country Planning Act 1990 to require local authorities, in drawing up their development plans, to have regard to environmental considerations, and to include policies for the conservation of the natural beauty and amenity of the land. PPG12 replaces two earlier PPGs: on local plans (former PPG12) and structure plans and regional guidance (former PPG15).

The new PPG includes an introductory paragraph on 'Planning and Sustainable Development' that links development plans to the objective of sustainable development:

> The planning system, and the preparation of development plans in particular, can contribute to the objectives of ensuring that development and growth are sustainable. The sum total of decisions in the planning field, as elsewhere, should not deny future generations the best of today's environment. This should be expressed through the policies adopted in development planning (DoE, 1992e).

The tenor of this paragraph is to emphasise the 'framework-setting' nature of development plans, and to set out the government's view that both development and growth need to be sustained and sustainable; but no further attempt is made to define these concepts. Nevertheless, the recognition that development planning has a role to play in meeting these objectives is important.

This role of plans is given further weight in the section on 'Plans and the Environment'. However, PPG12 gets into some difficulties in its advice on how plans should take environmental considerations into account. In the section on key strategic topics to be included in structure plans and Unitary Development Plans, the environment as such is not listed:

> Authorities should ensure that interactions between policies are fully considered; that the policies formulated under these headings form an integrated whole (for example, by forming an overall strategy for the coast); and that full account is taken of their economic, social and environmental effects. (So, the environment does not appear in the list as a key topic, because environmental considerations should be taken into account in drawing up *all* policies) (DoE, 1992e).

The PPG then amplifies the way in which this should occur:

> Most policies and proposals in all types of plan will have environmental implications, which should be appraised as part of the plan preparation process. Such an environmental appraisal is the process of identifying, quantifying, weighing up

and reporting on the environmental and other costs and benefits of the measures which are proposed. All the implications of the options should be analysed, including financial, social and environmental effects. A systematic appraisal ensures that the objectives of a policy are clearly laid out, and the trade-offs between options identified and assessed. Those who later interpret, implement and build on the policy will then have a clear record showing how the decision was made; in the case of development plans, this should be set out in the explanatory memorandum or reasoned justification. But the requirement to 'have regard' does not require a full environmental impact statement of the sort needed for projects likely to have serious environmental effects (DoE, 1992e).

Local planning authorities are also referred by the PPG to *Policy Appraisal and the Environment*:

> 'The guide may help authorities to introduce a commonly accepted and systematic approach to the treatment of environmental issues in developing their planning policies'.

Some local authorities – for instance Lancashire County Council and Solihull Metropolitan Borough Council – have already begun to take this on board, and many more can be expected to follow suit shortly. Appendix B.3 examines the benefits and limitations of PPG12.

Summary of UK government initiatives

The UK government seems to have taken an essentially compatible approach to both sustainable development and SEA, but appears to have carefully avoided linking the two concepts directly. As such, lacking the objective of sustainable development, *Policy Appraisal and the Environment* and PPG12 are limited to being a step up from project EIA. The strengths of *Policy Appraisal and the Environment* are in its clear exposition of possible methodologies for considering the impacts of policies: its requirements in terms of content, public participation and review are underdeveloped. PPG12 is commendable for its discussion of sustainability, its framework-setting approach, and its requirement for development plans to be subject to SEA; however the extent of its application has yet to be seen.

The procedures advocated by the proposed EC directive on SEA do not conflict with those of *Policy Appraisal and the Environment*, and in fact complement them. The emphasis of the guide is on methodology, while that of the proposed directive is on procedures. The guide is limited in its consideration of the issues, objectives, constraints and optionality of policies, whereas the proposed directive considers them quite thoroughly. On the other hand, the guide proposes a wide range of methods for valuing and comparing environmental resources and impacts, whereas the proposed directive scarcely touches on these methodological issues. Both emphasise the need to consider a variety of alternatives and to monitor the impacts of the policy, and both are limited in their consideration of the views of the public. The main area of contention in this respect is the UK government's unwillingness to be subject to an externally-imposed requirement to prepare SEAs. The proposed directive's requirement to show how environmental effects were taken into account when formulating the PPP's objectives is likely to be particularly unpopular.

3.5 Other countries

A number of other countries have instituted some form of SEA. In *Germany*, according to the federal regulation that implements Directive 85/337, EIAs must be carried out not only for projects, but also for construction guideline plans. These include binding land-use plans *(Bebauungsplan),*preparatory land-use plans *(Flächennutzungsplan)*, and regional plans (German Government, 1990; Wagner, 1992). However, the German government generally does not favour a formal system of SEA:

> The instruments of EIA are not appropriate for... the broad and abstractly-formulated goals of land-use planning. They may be appropriate for the goals of regional planning, providing these are very concretely formulated (roughly translated from Wagner, 1991b).

Most of the German regions *(Länder)* have developed administrative procedures for determining whether large projects are compatible with the aims and requirements of their spatial planning policies. These procedures may be extended to form the first tier in a two-tier EIA system; the second tier would involve the specific permit procedures for individual projects (UNECE, 1991a). Many communities and municipalities also prepare EIAs for their land-use plans on a voluntary basis. Other plans and programmes may include elements of EIA.

The German government and academic institutes are active in researching the feasibility of SEA (UVP Report, 1991). In particular, the Federal Ministry for Research and Technology is investigating the application of SEA to technology research projects; this is expected to lead to the development of a methodology for SEA of technology research projects, as well as an analysis of case studies (Kleinschmidt, 1991).

In *New Zealand* Part V of the Resource Management Act, which came into effect in October 1991, requires EIA of PPPs; it includes sections outlining the content of an SEA (Wells, 1991).

In *Canada* the Environment Minister tabled a motion in the House of Commons in June 1990 that would require the Cabinet to assess the environmental impacts of all its policy decisions; by late 1991, the proposal had not been agreed. The Federal Environmental Assessment Review Office at the time of writing is drafting guidelines for SEA (Couch, 1991).

In *Finland*

> Directives on legislative drafting are being supplemented with EIA regulations according to which environmental impacts will be assessed and taken into account in legislative drafts. The directives concerning the preparation of both central and local government action plans and budgets are being revised to include an obligation to assess the environmental impacts of the plans (UNECE, 1991a).

In *Japan*, guidelines prepared by the Ministry of Construction in 1985 require the preparation of city plans to be accompanied by, and coordinated with, an EIA (Barrett and Therivel, 1991). Regional Environmental Plans are also prepared, which address the environmental impacts of policies; however, these cannot be considered to be full SEAs.

Hong Kong does not have a formal SEA system. However, an SEA was prepared for the management of Deep Bay, a shallow coastal area near the border with China. Various uses of the bay were analysed, including increased disposal of sewage effluent, land reclamation, and maintenance of shellfish culture and wetlands. The SEA proposed guidelines for the management of Deep Bay, which are being used by a working party to coordinate development control around the bay (Montgomery, 1990).

3.6 International moves towards the implementation of strategic environmental assessment

A number of international organizations are also preparing SEAs, or considering doing so. Generally the function of these organizations is to give advice rather than to impose mandatory requirements. Several examples are given here, but they are by no means comprehensive.

UN Economic Commission for Europe (UNECE)

In 1990, the UNECE set up a task force to consider the extent to which EIA can be applied to PPPs. The task force looked at ten case studies of SEA in different countries, most of which relate to small-scale plans not very far removed from projects. For the most part, the case studies also consider environmental impacts within the context of existing political systems, rather than introducing a specific system of SEA. The task force has produced a report on these case studies with recommendations (Schrage, 1991; Braun, 1992).

In 1991, the UNECE also published a report on EIA, which recommended that:

> Priority should be accorded to the implementation of EIA through legislation which should... in the case of separate legislation, provide for linkage with other legislation... [and promote] integrated environmental management in relation to sustainable economic development...
> EIA legislation should apply to individual projects and could allow for appli-

cation to regional development schemes and programmes as well as general policies and strategies (UNECE, 1991a).

The UNECE Convention on Environmental Impact Assessment in a Transboundary Context (UNECE, 1991b) was signed by 28 countries and the EC in February 1991. It obliges parties to assess the environmental impacts of certain listed activities likely to cause significant adverse transboundary effects. It includes the following provision:

> Environmental impact assessment as required by this Convention shall, as a minimum requirement, be undertaken at the project level of the proposed activity. To the extent appropriate, the Parties shall endeavour to apply the principles of environmental impact assessment to policies, plans and programmes (UNECE, 1991b).

In January 1992, in response to a question about the implementation of the convention, Baroness Blatch noted that the convention had not yet entered into force but that the government 'are however committed to the integration of environmental concerns into policy appraisal and decision making' (House of Commons Official Report, 13 January 1992).

European Bank for Reconstruction and Development

The European Bank for Reconstruction and Development published EIA guidelines in 1992 that address the need for SEA:

> Regional and sectoral [EIAs] may be undertaken for development plans, sector-wide programmes, or multiple projects rather than single projects. Regional or sectoral [EIAs] can reduce the time and effort required for project-specific [EIAs] in the same region or sector by identifying issues, initiating baseline data collection and assembling existing data. In certain cases such [EIAs] could eliminate the need for a project-specific [EIA] altogether (EBRD, 1992).

To date, the European Bank has not yet prepared or commissioned any SEAs, but they are considering commissioning such work in the future (Murphy, 1992).

World Bank

The World Bank's Environmental Assessment Sourcebook of 1991 also discusses the need for SEA, claiming that it can reduce the time and effort required for project-specific EIAs by identifying issues, initiating the collection of baseline data, and assembling existing data (World Bank, 1991). The sourcebook also distinguishes between regional and sectoral assessments and discusses the objectives of these assessments.

The World Bank has already prepared, or is in the process of preparing, a number of SEAs, including:

- a regional SEA for the exploration and production of hydrocarbons in two coastal US states;

- a sectoral SEA of Pakistan's drainage programme;

- a sectoral SEA for a programme of road maintenance in Nigeria (see Box 3.4);

- a sectoral SEA for locust control in Africa (World Bank, 1991).

Box 3.4 SEA for road maintenance in Nigeria
(World Bank, 1991)

The Nigerian road network consists of interstate highways managed by the Federal Ministry of Works and Housing (FMWH), secondary roads managed by State Ministries of Works (SMOWs), and rural roads administered by Local Government Councils. International assistance has concentrated on rural roads in agricultural development projects and on the Federal highways. The state system includes 30,000 km of secondary roads, 10,000 km of which are paved. Many of them, constructed or last upgraded in the 1970s, urgently require rehabilitation followed by an effective programme of routine maintenance.

The Government of Nigeria is preparing a project for a five-year programme of road maintenance in selected states. It would finance repair of priority roads, paving of high-priority unsurfaced roads, routine maintenance, and institutional development and training components. The project is being prepared within FMWH, in collaboration with selected SMOWs.

An environmental reconnaissance was conducted by a consultant and staff members from FMWH and FEPA (the Nigerian Federal Environmental Protection Agency), to assist with project preparation. It established baseline conditions in the selected states, identified the environmental issues associated with road upgrading/rehabilitation and maintenance in each state, and recommended ways in which EIA could be incorporated into the project planning process. Recommendations included: (a) surveying and environmental screening and ranking of proposed subprojects; (b) preparation by FEPA of EIA guidelines for secondary roads; (c) preparation of EIAs for sub-projects likely to have a major impact; and (d) review and revision of standard contract specifications to require environmental safeguards, such as reseeding and embankment protection, and research by FMWH to propose measures to address the most important problems, such as gully erosion. The reconnaissance study also addressed the institutional capacity of FEPA, FMWH, and the SMOWs to carry out the work identified, and recommended various forms of training for staff in the relevant agencies.

3.7 Trends in systems of strategic environmental assessment

This section summarizes some of the trends, advantages and disadvantages of the existing and proposed SEA systems discussed above.

Who prepares the SEA?

Existing systems of SEA all require the agency that is concerned with setting the PPP also to prepare the SEA. For instance, the US Department of HUD prepares SEAs for projected metropolitan developments, and the US Department of Transportation prepares SEAs for radars at airports. The SEA may be incorporated into the primary document proposing the PPP, or as a separate document. In some cases, the SEA may be prepared with assistance from the agency in charge of environmental protection. For instance in the proposed Dutch SEA system, the National Environmental Protection Committee would provide assistance in preparing SEAs for PPPs with severe environmental repercussions, but not for less contentious PPPs.

Which PPPs require SEA?

The SEAs prepared to date are of three types: sectoral, regional and 'indirect'. The most commonly prepared or proposed sectoral SEAs include those for waste disposal, water supply, agriculture, forestry, energy, recreation, and transport. Less commonly, they are prepared for industry, housing and extraction. The most commonly prepared or proposed regional SEAs include those for regional plans, metropolitan/city plans, community plans, redevelopment plans and rural plans. Less commonly, they are prepared for airport plans, university plans, and other planning decisions concerning choices of locations for developments. Finally, the application of SEAs has been proposed for such 'indirect' PPPs as science and technology, financial/fiscal policies, and justice/enforcement.

It is noticeable that SEAs prepared to date have been carried out exclusively for plans and programmes, rather than for policies. The Netherlands' proposals for policy SEA are still in their early stages, and concern problems and issues in policy SEA rather than specific proposals for its implementation. This reflects the increasing complexity involved in applying a formal SEA procedure early in the policy-making process.

There seem to be two main methods for defining what kinds of PPPs may require SEA. The 'list method' gives a list of PPPs requiring SEA. For instance, the Dutch NEPP's Action A141 requires SEA for such listed topics as physical planning policy, housing and technology. The proposed EC directive on SEA also gives a list of PPPs. Such a list is generally clear and easy to understand, but may miss some PPPs that have a significant environmental impact. Alternatively, the 'definition method' gives a definition of PPPs requiring SEA, but does not specifically list them. For instance, in California and in the US national EIA system, SEA is required for projects that are linked geographically, as logical parts in a chain of actions, etc. This method is likely to be more comprehensive, but determination of which PPPs require SEA becomes more difficult.

Content of the SEA

From the few established SEA systems in existence, it is possible to suggest the likely content required by future SEA systems:

- table of contents;
- summary;
- description of the proposed PPP and its objectives;
- description of the need for, and feasibility of, the PPP;
- alternatives to the PPP;
- description of 'boundaries' – regional or sectoral – that form the limits of the SEA;
- relation to other relevant PPPs and environmental requirements;
- scoping of issues/impacts to which the SEA is limited (including a statement explaining why other possible issues/impacts are not addressed);
- description of affected environment;
- environmental consequences of the proposed PPP and alternatives;
- impact evaluation;
- proposed mitigation measures;
- recommendations;
- list of preparers and recipients.

None of the SEAs seen by the authors include all of these points, but they all address most of them.

Impacts considered in SEA

The impacts that could be considered in an SEA can be divided into three types. 'Traditional' impacts are impacts that would already be covered by most project EIAs, such as water quality, air quality, geology and noise. 'Sustainability-related' impacts specifically consider resources that are threatened by irreversible, cumulative or secondary impacts: examples include unique natural features, significant habitats and species, use of energy, and use of non-renewable resources. Finally, 'policy-related' impacts are affected by, and affect, other policies; these include safety and risk, suitability of development, climatic and fire hazards and social conditions.

   The proposed EC directive also lists the impacts that should be considered in an SEA: this list is similar to that of Directive 85/337, and covers only 'traditional' impacts. The US Department of HUD's list of impacts that an SEA has to address is more comprehensive, including traditional, sustainability-related and policy-related impacts. However, it addresses sustainability itself only slightly; sustainability as such was not yet a central issue in 1981, when the HUD's manual was prepared. The Netherlands uses sustainability-related issues in its methodology for screening government policy areas. Other systems do not give a formal list of impacts that must be addressed.

SEA methodology

There are few officially-acknowledged methodologies for SEA. The US Department of HUD has produced a formal SEA manual, which gives clear step-by-step instructions for carrying out an areawide environmental appraisal. The UK's guidebook on policy appraisal reviews techniques for assigning monetary values to environmental assets and impacts. The Canadian government is preparing guidelines for the preparation of SEA. The proposed EC directive lists methods for SEA, broken down into their functions, e.g. to help in deciding if an assessment is necessary, in identifying impacts, or in predicting impacts. A number of computer models and other methods for SEA have been prepared by academic and research institutions. Examples include the computer model 'Strategic Environmental Assessment System' (Ratick and Lakshamanan, 1983), and various methodologies established by German researchers (UVP Report, 1991). Overall, however, SEA has been considered much more on the theoretical than the practical level, and SEA methodologies are neither well-developed nor commonly agreed upon. Appendix C discusses SEA methodology at greater length.

Public consultation and participation

The level of public consultation and participation that should be required by an SEA system has obviously been an issue of concern. Public participation in the preparation of PPPs is complicated by the breadth of issues involved, the difficulty of arranging meetings between the various types of public involved and the appropriate level of decision-makers, and the frequent lack of a specific point in time when a decision regarding the PPP is made. Nevertheless, some SEA systems require public participation. In California, for instance, public comments are sought for both the draft SEA and the final SEA. In the Netherlands, public consultation and participation is widespread, and public inquiries are held.

Decisions based on SEA

The audience for existing SEAs has traditionally been the government agency that decides on the PPP. In some cases, an independent environmental authority comments on, or assists in the preparation of, the SEA. Review by an independent environmental authority has the advantage of ensuring that the SEA is comprehensive, accurate and unbiased. Its disadvantages are that such a review takes time and effort, and may lead to antagonism between agencies. The SEA systems of the Netherlands and the US are examples of an independent environmental agency being involved in the SEA in every case. In Germany, most plans are reviewed by independent environmental bodies, while in France and Italy, only a few plans are reviewed. In other countries, including Spain, Portugal and the UK, no such body exists (although in the UK a review function is offered on a private basis by the Institute of Environmental Assessment).

This chapter has shown the wide variety of possible SEA systems. Some have existed for decades, while others have yet to be agreed upon. Some emphasize methodologies, others are primarily procedural. Some cover a wide range of PPPs, while others are limited to only a few. Arguably the most important difference between these systems, however, is between those that 'trickle down' the concept of sustainability, and those that build up from project EIA. This will be discussed further in Chapter 7. The next chapters review the need for, and possible applications of, SEA in the UK.

Notes

1. For instance Save the Yaak Committee v. Block, 840 F.2d 714 (9th Cir. 1988); Conner v. Burford, 348 F.2d 1441 (9th Cir. 1988); LaFlamme v. FERC 852 F.2d 389 (9th Cir. 1988); City of Tenakee Springs v. Clough, 915 F.2d 1308 (9th Cir. 1990).

4:

Coastal zones

This chapter presents the first of three case studies exploring the need for, and applicability of, SEA in selected situations in the UK. It considers one particular bio-geographical zone, namely the coast. Chapter 5 considers the energy sector and chapter 6 a habitat, lowland heath. These case studies exemplify some of the inadequacies in the current system that strategic environmental assessment would help to rectify, as well as some of the likely difficulties that would be faced in its implementation.

Firstly the importance of coastal zones and the threats that they face are set out. Existing international, national and regional policies affecting coastal zones are then discussed. A review of EIAs for projects on the coast shows that the existing system of project EIA does not adequately cover all of the impacts of development projects on coastlines. These results point to the need for a more strategic approach to managing coastal zones; the chapter concludes with a discussion of the factors that such a strategic approach must consider.

4.1 The importance of coastal zones

The UK has more than 15,000 km of coastline and approximately 300,000 km^2 of territorial waters. Three-quarters of its counties/regions border the coast (Gubbay,1990). Many types of habitats are associated with the coast. These provide refuges for many key species of the UK's native fauna, and in particular for nationally and internationally important populations of wading birds and wildfowl. The UK coastline is also important because its location and climate enable it to provide a home for a number of temperate, Mediterranean and Arctic species of flora and fauna.

The UK's many estuaries are particularly important for both their conservation and their economic value: they are among the most biologically productive ecosystems in the world. As well as providing a vital feeding and nesting ground for bird species these areas are used as nurseries by many commercially exploited fish stocks, particularly plaice and sole, thus contributing to the North Sea's reputation as the most profitable sea in the world.

4.2 Threats to coastal zones

There are many threats to coastlines generally, and to estuaries in particular. Large inter-tidal areas have been lost in the past, notably the reduction of the Tees estuary by about 90 per cent in the last 100 years as a result of industrial development. Today more piecemeal developments still have the overall effect of fragmenting habitats and causing large-scale cumulative losses. Notable controversies have concerned land claim on the Ribble and Wash estuaries, a port development at Felixstowe, and the Cardiff Bay barrage. In the south-east of England, natural subsidence and the possibility of rising sea-levels further threaten intertidal land (RSPB, 1991a). A survey carried out by the RSPB (Rothwell and Housden, 1990) showed that of 123 estuaries examined, 80 (65 per cent) were under some degree of threat, and 43 (35 per cent) were in imminent danger of permanent damage. A wide range of threats was identified, but recreational pressures, marinas, pollution, land claim and barrage schemes featured especially prominently. In 1992 the exercise was repeated: of 126 estuaries examined, 57 (45 per cent) faced threats of permanent damage, mainly from marina developments, land claim, port expansion, pollution, recreational pressures, bait digging and cockle fishing. All these threats had increased in number since the initial survey in 1988.

Energy-related developments on the coast take many forms, including power stations, barrages, and gas terminals and pipelines. Of these, power stations are the most common, and barrages the most destructive. General problems of energy-related developments are discussed in chapter 5.

Perhaps the most controversial type of coast-based energy development are the barrages that are proposed for the harnessing of tidal power. Several sites for tidal barrage schemes are under review at the time of writing, including those at the Mersey Estuary, Severn Estuary, Duddon (Cumbria), and on the Wyre (Lancashire). These barrage schemes are 'permeable', in that they would still leave a tidal regime, but in a much reduced form. This has several implications for the estuarine ecosystem. The exposed feeding area for birds (mudflats, etc.) is reduced, so the site would not be able to support the numbers of birds it did before the barrage. The high water tide mark would reposition lower down the shore, with terrestrial vegetation advancing, again removing habitat for fish and birds. In many schemes the water would cover the intertidal areas for longer periods, further reducing feeding time and area. With water not being allowed to reach the upper levels of saltmarshes, the seeds produced by the salt-marsh vegetation would be prevented from being washed into the feeding zone of the birds and fish. Rates and patterns of erosion and sedimentation would tend to be drastically changed, with a substantial lowering of salinity behind the barrage also likely.

In many places the normal forces of waves and tides require the construction of *coastal defence works*. Any future rises in sea level will result in some loss of both intertidal area and shoreline, and extra coastal protection works to combat the rise in sea level may themselves have a major impact on flora and fauna. Such work may be detrimental to wildlife in 'fossilising' the existing coastline, owing to the loss of intertidal habitats becoming 'squeezed' between hard high-tide defences and rising low-tide levels. Fragmentation of marsh habitats can occur behind sea walls when farmers improve drainage in order to minimize winter floods and lower summer water levels (RSPB,1991a).

The Government has outlined a strategy to combat sea level rise by refurbishing defences to reduce existing risk, while continuing research into coastal processes, climate, and future policy (MAFF, 1991b). The Government is also attempting to reconcile these aims with the requirements of coastal conservation. In late 1991, the Ministry of Agriculture, Fisheries and Food reviewed the environmental conservation aspects of flood and coastal defence, with the aim of developing a national strategy for these works (MAFF, 1991a). However, grant aid gives priority to those schemes that protect property and people, not flora and fauna; this does not give adequate weighting to ecological factors. These tend to be addressed when they can support other primary aims: for instance the MAFF noted that a coastal defence scheme at Aldeburgh, Suffolk, could not have been justified on urban and agricultural benefits alone, so environmental and recreational benefits were also considered (MAFF, 1991a).

A major problem linked to coastal defence is that of *land reclamation*, formerly for agriculture and now for development. This has resulted in extensive losses of internationally important intertidal and salt-marsh habitats, especially in the south and east of England where the largest tracts were once found. In 1989 the then Nature Conservancy Council (NCC) found that at least 50 estuaries were subject to at least one proposal involving land claim (NCC, 1989).

Heavy industry has traditionally favoured coastal areas, because they are easily accessible and because in the past coastal waters have provided a free disposal site for waste products. Several pollution incidents have occurred over the years in prime estuary sites. In the late 1970s hundreds of birds were killed in the Mersey after ingesting organic lead from petrochemical works in the estuary. The Mersey and Southampton Water are both estuaries that have been subject to oil spills (Rothwell and Housden, 1990). The levels and types of industrial discharge are under tighter control today, but many water bodies still suffer from years of uncontrolled discharge: the Mersey, Tees, Thames and Taff, which all have substantial estuarine areas, are still very heavily polluted.

Pressures on coastlines from *recreational activities* are increasing, as more people with more leisure time are becoming interested in water-borne pursuits such as small vessel sailing, windsurfing and jet-skiing. Some of these activities are problematic for wildlife because of the disturbance they cause, to birds in particular.

The demand for marinas is growing particularly quickly. At the time of writing there are 154 marinas in estuaries around the UK, 78 more are proposed, and estimates are that demand will rise by 40-50 per cent by the year 2000 (NCC, 1989; Sidaway, 1991). The problem is most marked along the popular stretches of coast in the south and south-east of England. Marinas illustrate particularly well the lack of strategic planning for coastlines where individual proposals are addressed in isolation and without any consideration of the contribution they make to actual demand when set against proposals elsewhere.

Recreation-oriented barrage schemes, i.e. those that are not designed to harness power, but are constructed purely for amenity reasons, also have a strong impact on coastlines. These developments take the form of impermeable barriers that provide static water for water sports and (supposedly) aesthetically pleasing settings for waterside developments. Impermeable barrages remove all tidal movement, impounding water behind the barrier usually at or near the former high tide level. This permanently floods all the intertidal feeding areas which may once have been present there. In 1990, 22 estuarine sites had been the subject of preliminary investigation for either permeable (usually energy-related) or impermeable barrage construction (Rothwell and Housden, 1990). Impermeable barrages are not well developed, yet proposals are under consideration for the Taff/Ely estuary, and for the Usk and the Tees.

Finally, *fish farming* also illustrates the problems associated with the current planning and administration of coastlines. Marine fish farming began about 25 years ago, but has grown rapidly since then, and is now a major rural industry. The great majority of fish farms are located on the clean and varied tidal coasts of Scotland. Scotland currently produces about 18 per cent of the world's output of salmon; in 1991, 327 leases had been granted for salmon farms and 382 leases existed for shellfish farms in Scotland (Scottish Office, 1991). The fish farming sector is financially assisted by both Highlands and Islands Enterprise and the Agricultural Development programme for Orkney, Shetland and the Inner Isles.

Fish farming has a number of impacts on the coastal environment. These include impacts on water quality, coastal ecology, visual amenity, existing infrastructure, and existing fish farms. Fish farming also has cumulative, synergistic and secondary impacts over and above its local individual impacts. The cumulative impacts of the chemicals used in fish farming can have deleterious impacts on both human health and ecosystem quality. For instance sea lice, which are a major problem on fish farms, are controlled by using the chemical 'Nuvan'. Nuvan's active ingredient is dichlorvos, which is on the Government's Red List of Dangerous Substances. It is also on the North Sea States' Priority Hazardous Substances List, for which a 50 per cent reduction of inputs compared to 1985 levels is planned for 1995. One source has calculated that, unless an alternative is found, inputs of the chemical from salmon farming alone may have increased by 700 per cent in that period (SWCL, 1990). Similarly, antibiotics which are used to treat fish diseases may affect the local benthic fauna.

Salmon farms present problems for wild salmon populations by subjecting them to increased levels of pollution and parasite infestation. Cage-reared stock can breed with wild stock, which interferes with the latter's genetic integrity, and may affect its ability to return to specific river systems during breeding time.

An indirect impact of fish farms is related to the feedstock used. The industry relies heavily on high protein feeds, often in the form of other fish, particularly capelin, sprat and sand-eels. Even if the use of these feedstock fish is reduced in the future, the salmon will still need to be fed; the food will most likely be in the form of other fish but obtained from further afield. Salmon farming is thus likely to contribute to the over-fishing of other fish species, rather than providing a long-term substitute for over-fished wild stocks of salmon (SWCL, 1990).

In 1989 the Crown Estates Commission published guidelines on fish farming in Scotland (CECb, 1989). This document appears to give a green light for the industry to develop without any strategic guidance on how to deal with its possible environmental impacts. Scottish Wildlife and Countryside Link note that:

> The total absence of a conservation strategy for coastal ecosystems, and the lack of a neutral authority, remain as major flaws in any claim by the Government to be pursuing an environmentally responsible policy in fish farming... Precautionary safeguards on development should be designed to protect ecosystems of known or suspected vulnerability, and should be introduced without delay, to remain in place until superseded by protective measures based on adequate research (SWCL, 1990).

4.3 Policies regarding coastal zones

International legislation

A number of conventions, directives and designations offering protection to the coastal zone have been agreed. The Council of Europe's 1979 Convention on the Conservation of European Wildlife and Natural Habitats (the 'Berne Convention') requires signatory nations to conserve their populations of wild flora and fauna species (including migratory species, endangered and vulnerable species, and marine wildlife), and habitats. The UK Government ratified the Convention in 1982.

The Convention on the Conservation of Migratory Species of Wild Animals (the 'Bonn Convention') requires strict protection for a number of listed endangered animals. It also covers specific aspects of the species' conservation, including management, hunting, and research. The UK signed the Convention in 1979, and it was ratified in 1985.

The Convention Concerning the Protection of the World Cultural and Natural Heritage (the 'World Heritage Convention') was adopted under the auspices of UNESCO in 1972, and ratified by the UK in 1984. It aims to identify and protect sites that are of such unique value that they form part of the world's cultural or natural heritage. Of the UK's 14 heritage sites, 3 are natural heritage sites, and 11 are cultural heritage sites (NCC, 1991).

Biosphere Reserves were first proposed by UNESCO's Man and the Biosphere Programme in 1974 as areas of land forming a worldwide network of sites, linked by common international standards and protected for conservation purposes and scientific information exchange. The UK has 13 Biosphere Reserves, which are also National Nature Reserves; they were designated in 1976 and 1977 (NCC, 1991).

The Convention on Wetlands of International Importance Especially as Waterfowl Habitat (the 'Ramsar Convention') was the first treaty to concern itself exclusively with habitat conservation. It was agreed in 1971 and ratified by the UK in 1976. The main obligations are to designate suitable wetlands for inclusion in the List of Wetlands of International Importance; promote the conservation of wetlands and, as far as possible, their wise use; and establish nature reserves on wetlands. In the UK, as at August 1992, there are 54 Ramsar sites and approximately 100 candidate sites.

EC Directive 79/409 on the Conservation of Wild Birds (the 'Birds Directive') requires the establishment of a network of Special Protection Areas (SPAs) throughout the EC, and other measures for the protection of wild bird populations and their habitats. As at August 1992 the UK has designated 54 sites as SPAs. Of 155 estuary sites in the UK, 68 qualify as Ramsar sites and/or SPAs. Neither the Birds Directive nor the Ramsar Convention precludes the use of wetlands for human activity, but tests must be met according to whether the activity will lead to the deterioration of existing habitats.

EC Directive 85/337 requires the preparation of EIAs for a number of developments that are likely to take place on coasts (see Appendix A.1). These include ports and inland waterways under Annex I, and water management projects for agriculture, salmon breeding, reclamation of land from the sea (for agriculture), mineral extraction, harbour construction, canalization and flood relief works, marinas, dams and waste water treatment plants under Annex II. Other projects not specifically related to coasts also require EIA. In some of these cases the UK may not be in compliance with the directive. One example is its lack of specific EIA regulations concerning marine dredging for minerals and for offshore hydrocarbon developments required under Annex II. There is also a lack of conformity between the different language versions of the Directive, where the UK translation refers to salmon, while other member states refer to salmonids (Wathern, 1988). Measures to rectify these problems are under consideration by the Government at the time of writing.

The EC's Directorate-General XI is currently preparing a strategy for the EC's coastal areas. Possible aspects of this may include an observatory of coastal areas to exchange information; better coastal planning, including threshold criteria for such factors as economic development and planning permission; and a proposal for legal instruments requiring the preparation of a strategic plan for each coastal area (European Information Service, 1991).

The House of Commons Select Committee on the Environment reporting to the government on Coastal Protection and Planning in July 1992 recommended:

> ...that the Government take every opportunity to involve United Kingdom experts in the formulation and discussion of proposed EC policies and Directives on the coastal zone, and we urge the Government to put pressure on the Commission to make progress with an EC Directive on coasts (HOC Environment Committee, 1992).

At the time of writing the European Commission has not yet published its proposals for a Community strategy for integrated coastal zone management, although an initiative is programmed in the Fifth Environmental Action Programme.

In addition, EC Directive 92/43 on the Conservation of Natural and Semi-Natural Habitats and of Wild Flora and Fauna ('the Habitats Directive') requires the establishment of a European Network of special protection zones called 'Natura 2000', whose aim is to ensure the conservation of threatened species and threatened types of habitats in the EC. This directive should bring about further protection for coastal and estuarine habitats.

Finally, pollution law affects estuarine and coastal water quality, and coastal developments. For example the ministerial declaration of the third North Sea Conference of 1990 continued a series of agreements aimed at reducing and ultimately eliminating pollution from the North Sea. The UK committed itself in 1987 to achieving a 50 per cent reduction, between 1985 and 1995, of inputs of substances that are persistent, toxic and liable to bioaccumulation. The EC Directive 76/160 on the Quality of Bathing Water requires improvements in sewage treatment and the use of long sea outfalls. This has the benefit of improving water standards, but may also have the effect of bringing about further developments on the coast.

UK government policies

The Department of the Environment published a draft Planning Policy Guidance note on coastal planning in March 1992 (DoE, 1992c). The draft PPG defines the coast as an important multi-faceted national resource on which a range of activities take place, and which contains certain unique habitats and landscapes. It advises on how planning authorities should attempt to reconcile the needs of development with those of the landscape, conservation interests and recreation. (It has since been published as PPG 20.)

The document notes that local authorities, when making planning decisions, should consider the impact of onshore developments on offshore locations and vice versa, impacts linked to developments spanning the mean low-water mark (marinas, harbours and barrages), the cumulative impacts of smaller developments as well as the direct impacts of large development proposals, the possible impacts of developments outside their immediate boundaries, and the sensitive nature of some proposed sites such as wetlands and estuaries.

The PPG also discusses developments that tend to favour coastal locations – marinas and harbours, mineral extraction, large-scale developments, and energy projects. It establishes policies for dealing with risks of flooding, erosion and land instability, and suggests that areas most likely to be at risk be identified, within which policies should be adopted that restrict development. On low-lying undeveloped coasts a 'managed retreat' of the upper shoreline may be most appropriate to accommodate rising sea-levels or increased flooding, for example.

The PPG views planning for development of the coast as having a strong strategic dimension because of the extent of the coastline and cross-boundary issues. It highlights the need for consistency in coastal policy and in the preparation of structure plans to prevent conflict over cross-boundary issues such as up- or down-stream effects of development on habitats. A list is given of information that local authorities should consider when preparing development plans, and this specifies information on particularly sensitive coastal areas. It refers to PPG12, which identifies topics that structure plans should cover, and which promotes the adoption of an integrated approach to such areas as coastlines (see Appendix B.3 for a discussion of the extent to which the PPG actually achieves this).

Regional and local policies

A number of local authorities have made efforts to establish management initiatives for those areas of coastline within their jurisdiction. A recent survey (Devon County Council, 1992) of the estuary and coastal management initiatives of 106 coast-based district councils identified very varied levels of involvement. Of the 67 district councils that responded to the survey, 29 (43 per cent) were involved in 'multi-parameter' management initiatives, 6 (9 per cent) planned to be involved in multi-parameter management initiatives, 11 (17 per cent) were involved in single parameter management initiatives, and 21 (31 per cent) had no involvement in coastal initiatives. This indicates a high awareness of, and concern about, coastal management (Devon CC, 1992).

A number of initiatives at county or similar levels for coastline protection and management are also taking place. These include a management plan for the Mersey and a proposed plan for the Dee Estuary, a management plan for the Tees Estuary, a management plan for Poole Harbour, Hampshire County Council's proposed management plans for the Solent, a proposed management plan for the Heritage Coasts in Kent, Norfolk and South Glamorgan, Northumberland's Coastal Management Plan, a management plan for a number of Suffolk's coastal areas, management plans for the Neath Estuary and Crymlyn Bay, and a management plan for Chichester Harbour. Several of these plans, notably those of Cheshire, Cleveland, Norfolk, Northumberland and West Glamorgan have required extensive consultation and cooperation with other authorities (Devon CC, 1992).

The Scottish Regional Councils have also developed coastal strategies. For instance, Borders Regional Council at the time of writing is developing a management plan that will tie in with the Northumberland Coastal Management Plan, and through which it aims to provide a coordinated cross-border management framework for the whole of the Borders coastline. The regional council is also a leading member of the Tweed Forum which aims to coordinate the variety of interests within the River Tweed catchment area. Highland Regional Council has produced a document that highlights the coastal zone as an area in which careful planning is necessary, and the council also has a working party on fish farms that produces policy reports on aquaculture (Devon CC, 1992).

Box 4.1 gives an example of a particularly successful local authority management plan for coastlines.

Other organisations' policies

A wide range of other organizations have an interest in coastal areas and in the formulation and implementation of related management documents. For instance the RSPB are currently involved in a pilot scheme to develop a coastal strategy for the north-west of England: the project focuses on the Mersey and Ribble estuaries, and Morecambe Bay, and aims to counteract problems arising from the inadequate legislative and administrative framework for coastal zones. The National Rivers Authority (NRA) coordinates a wide range of water-based management initiatives. It has recently set up a pilot scheme in its Welsh Region to produce management plans for river catchments. The plans are drawn up in consultation with the other interested parties to 'represent an agreed multi-functional strategy for realizing the environmental potential of the catchment concerned' (Devon CC, 1992). On the basis of the Welsh framework the NRA's South West Region has produced a draft catchment management plan for the Taw/Torridge Estuary.

4.4 EIAs of projects affecting coastal zones

Of 253 EISs prepared in the UK between 1988 and early 1992 and held at Oxford Polytechnic, 35 (14%) related to proposed developments on the coast. These included 16 energy-related projects, 5 leisure developments, 4 flood defence works, and 4 water or sewage treatment works. Other developments included harbours, an incinerator, and a fish farm. Table 4.1 summarises the development types and locations.

Box 4.1 Sefton Metropolitan Borough Council's coastal management plan
(Devon CC, 1992)

The Sefton Coast Management Plan is an example of the way in which the needs of an area of coastline can be viewed strategically. Sefton Metropolitan Borough Council manages 35km of coastline, which is dominated by an extensive dune system. Its coastal management plan was initially developed to preserve this habitat type, but it has subsequently expanded to cover many other aspects of the coastline. The management plan is based on the Heritage Coast model and involves a wide range of consulting agencies. Nature conservation is covered by local designations such as Local Nature Reserves.

The management plan is administered by a working party that aims to represent all the major interested parties within Sefton. A coastal management officer has been appointed. The working party advises a steering group which makes and implements decisions within the context of the plan. The steering group and working party have no statutory planning powers, although any planning applications which may affect the scheme are referred to the project officer for comment, and the objectives of the management plan have been incorporated into the Borough Unitary Development Plan.

The management plan is primarily funded by the borough council. It employs eight full-time people, and ten additional full-time equivalents in specialist areas such as recreation, planning and tourism. It has generated a large amount of data about management techniques, flora and fauna, and the physical processes at work in respect of the sand dune systems. The possibility of incorporating these data into a geographical information system (GIS) is being investigated. Good consultation between the working party, steering group and the interested parties, and significant capital outlay are making a valuable contribution to the protection of this area of internationally important habitat.

An assessment of the overall quality of the EISs according to recognized review criteria (Lee and Colley, 1990) revealed that about 40 per cent of them were generally good (particularly those for the energy sector), one-third were adequate, and the rest were poor. However, even the relatively good ones failed to address any cumulative impacts that the development would have on the environment. Some statements acknowledged this limitation, one for instance noting that:

Each component is being considered separately for the purposes of [EIA], with individual planning applications submitted to the relevant authorities. This is because each component is being constructed by different companies and/or their planning applications or construction schedules do not allow combination into a single [EIS] (Teesside Power Ltd, 1990).

Table 4.1 **Summary of EIAs regarding the coastal zone**

Location	Number	Proposed development
Fife	1	Harbour
Tees Estuary	4	Incinerator Pipeline (x2) Gas processing plant
Humber	2	Power station (x2)
East Anglia	4	Flood defence Sewage treatment works Port Harbour expansion
Thames	1	Flood defence
Medway	1	Marina
Folkestone	1	Oil exploration
Solent	4	Power station Leisure Marina Barrage
Taw/Torridge	2	Flood defence Power station
Severn	4	Reclamation Energy Harbour Incinerator
Milford Haven	1	Pipeline
Conwy	1	Marina
Dee	5	Coal tip Flood defence Power station River crossing Road
Lancashire coast	3	Gas terminal Treatment works (x2)
West coast of Scotland	1	Fish farm

One EIS mentioned other developments that had taken place, or were proposed, in the wider area, but failed to consider the possible cumulative impacts of these. Another recognized that the proposed development would take place on a major estuarine complex, but did not address cumulative impacts. In general most EISs reviewed the impact that they would have in isolation, and assumed that other developments on the coast or estuary were static.

Some of the locations of the proposed developments, summarized in Table 4.1, exemplify well the need to consider cumulative impacts. The Dee Estuary is subject to a variety of pressures from a power station, pipelines, a coal tip, a river crossing, and a flood defence project. This is in spite of the various designations and nature reserves being present, including Ramsar site, Special Protection Area, Site of Special Scientific Interest, Local Nature Reserve and RSPB reserve. The Dee Estuary can also be regarded as one part of the coastal complex encompassing the Mersey, the Ribble and Morecambe Bay: developments are being proposed at all of these locations.

This analysis highlights two major issues. First, EIAs are not adequately considering the cumulative impact of proposed developments. Although EC Directive 85/337 requires cumulative impacts to be addressed (see Appendix A.2), this has proven to be the exception rather than the rule with respect to coastal developments in the UK. Second, statutory site safeguard measures do not provide adequate safeguards for the fragile and rapidly-diminishing coastal ecosystems. Damaging developments are still being proposed, and approved, for areas designated for nature conservation purposes. SEA could be a useful tool in ensuring that these biogeographical units are afforded greater protection. This is discussed in the next section.

4.5 The need for strategic environmental assessment

Despite numerous mechanisms established for the protection of coastlines and the application of EIA to some proposed development projects, the UK's internationally important coastal zone resources are diminishing rather than increasing (NCC, 1991). Even within designated sites, habitat loss is continuing: 26 estuaries in the Ramsar/SPA network have suffered recent losses, 21 losing intertidal/subtidal areas, and over 50 per cent of internationally important estuaries face the threat of losses by direct land claim (NCC, 1991).

Reports from both government and non-governmental organisations confirm that coastal management practices are poor and that there is a need for better coordination and guidelines. The Countryside Commission's (1991) report on Heritage Coast matters calls for management of the wider coastline and states that 'what is missing is a national policy framework for the coast as a whole'. The then NCC also favoured the idea in its estuaries review (1991), stating that 'integrated coastal zone management can help save the remaining estuaries and their wildlife by treating them as functional units'. The Government's Planning Policy Guidance Note on Coastal Planning is an encouraging step forward, but the 1990 White Paper on the Environment does not propose a strategic plan for the coastal zone.

An initial issue (although one that has been exaggerated as a reason for not making faster progress) in the application of SEA to coastlines, is to define where the coastal zone begins and ends. At present, there is no definition of the 'coastal zone'. Coasts certainly include a landward component, a marine component, and the inter-tidal area, but any existing working definitions are based on a combination of administrative, practical, economic and environmental factors. The PPG on coastal planning (in draft at the time of writing) defines the coastal zone as the area extending seawards and landwards from the coastlines, where land and marine influences interact. This allows some scope for developers to challenge the interpretation adopted by particular local authorities. A report from the Marine Conservation Society (Gubbay, 1990) suggests that the seaward boundary should correspond with the 12 nautical mile limit of UK territorial waters. Inland boundaries are harder to define because of the many administrative boundaries. In Heritage Coasts the main factors determining inland boundaries are topography and land use.

At present, some management and planning initiatives are already in operation at local, regional and national level, and these provide useful examples of both the advantages and difficulties of establishing an SEA system for coasts. However these tend to deal with particular uses of the coast rather than all of the uses, or with very specific areas of coastline. The biggest gap appears at the national level where those initiatives that do operate (Preferred Conservation Zones and Preferred Development Zones for the oil and gas industries) are not concerned with integrating all uses of the coastal area. It is at this level that attention must be focused for truly strategic planning for coasts. Many government departments, statutory bodies and other groups have statutory duties and powers related to coastlines. This is a particularly acute cause of the failure of strategic overviews of the coast, and confusion is caused by apparently overlapping jurisdictions (RSPB, 1991).

Policies and management plans at a local level need to be linked together by regional and national policy frameworks. The incremental linking of regional coastal plans, such as those of Northumberland and the Borders Region, is one way of moving from the local to the regional level in ensuring that management policies are consistent and conflict can be minimized. A national framework, financial support, and integration for management at local and regional levels is needed.

Despite increased awareness of the problems development activities cause, coastlines and their associated habitats are still under threat. Sustainability and the precautionary principle are missing from the coastal planning PPG. In July 1992 the House of Commons Select Committee on the Environment reported on its inquiry into Coastal Zone Protection and Planning. The committee stated:

> We believe there is a need to establish a national framework for the strategic planning of the United Kingdom coast, urged on by forthcoming EC legislation.

We recommend that the Government considers how best to formulate a national strategy that sets long-term objectives and guidelines for implementing coastal policy.

The committee noted that the process of EIA for coastal-based developments is currently under review in certain respects. Directive 85/337 is at present being implemented in the UK by integrating its requirements with existing development consent procedures. EIA is required for a wide range of projects in the coastal zone that are likely to have significant environmental effects. However, the government recognizes that the application of EIA in coastal areas could be improved. In consequence, at the time of writing the government:

- is considering whether to use the power of section 70A of the Town and Country Planning Act 1990 to add coastal protection works to Schedule 2 of the Town and Country Planning (Assessment of Environmental Effects) Regulations 1988 so that EIA would be required where such works were likely to have significant effects;

- is reviewing permitted development rights accorded to port and harbour developers and other bodies on the coast as part of a wider consideration of the classes of permitted development in Schedule 2 to the General Development Order;

- is proposing to review the 'Government Review Procedure' for the extraction of marine aggregates, including the procedures for EIA.

In its report the Select Committee concluded:

We recommend the Government review the application of procedures for [EIA] within the coastal zone in order to ensure a more equitable and comprehensive coverage of the requirements. We also recommend that the Government urge the EC to review the scope of Directive 85/337/EEC with respect to the coastal zone.

EC initiatives for both SEA and integrated coastal zone management have been proposed, but these are advancing only slowly. The UK government's decision to produce a PPG note on coastal planning is a positive step forward. However, the PPG is no substitute for a national coastal strategy and is a long way short of a comprehensive vehicle for promoting more sustainable use of the coastline.

5:

Energy sector

This chapter examines energy policy in the UK for any evidence of existing practice in applying EIA at the strategic level, and considers the future scope within the energy sector for this. The sector was chosen as a case study because of its importance in environmental, economic and political terms. Its importance and complexity make it a necessary complement to the other case studies, in that there is little evidence from our review of existing systems of SEA of its application to a whole sector (see Chapter 3). This complexity, of course, presents problems for analysis; this study therefore concentrates on an overview of national policy, followed by an examination of existing practice and the scope for the introduction of SEA in case examples of plans, programmes and projects.

5.1 The importance of the energy sector

Energy is a sector of major importance to national and global economies. It is important in its own right as an element of national production, as an essential input to other sectors in national economies (such as transport and manufacturing), and as a component of domestic or household activities (OECD, 1991). The sector has also major significance in global economic and political terms as a tradeable resource. In addition to the traditional concerns of governments about energy security and the relationship of energy supply with economic growth, attention has also been paid recently to the environmental impacts of the sector, especially since the work of the Intergovernmental Panel on Climate Change (IPCC) has pointed to the major contribution of energy-related activity to global warming and emissions to the atmosphere (Houghton et al, 1990).

These studies also forecast imminent changes in the energy sector, related not just to the increasing importance of environmental objectives in determining energy policies, but also to the increasing share of energy demand of the developing world relative to that of industrialized countries (International Energy Agency, 1992). In the developed world, there has been a decoupling of energy consumption and growth in terms of GDP (the seven largest OECD economies experienced a 26 per cent increase in energy requirements over the period 1970 to 1988, while sustaining a 73 per cent growth of GDP), and it seems possible that, in these economies, we are approaching a threshold where conventional fuels may be displaced by new and/or renewable sources of energy, or increased efficiency of energy use. The concern is no longer with the imminent depletion of conventional fuels (indeed, there may be more potentially exploitable reserves), but with the cumulative environmental impacts of their exploitation. Conventional fuels are not likely to lose their relative importance in the next 20 to 25 years, but, with the need for stabilization of carbon emissions and greenhouse gases, a major reassessment of energy policies is being advocated (Strong, 1992).

Moreover, developments that produce and use energy have local impacts as well as the regional and global ones referred to above. A key element of the introduction of new or alternative sources of energy should be the establishment of a framework to consider all of these impacts. An indication of the energy sector's current importance within the UK as a source of major development projects is shown by the estimate that about 20 per cent of the EISs prepared in the UK since 1988 (under the 1988 Environmental Assessment Regulations) relate to energy production, even though this excludes energy conservation projects, small-scale energy projects, and other energy projects not covered by EC Directive 85/337.

5.2 National policy

An initial difficulty in considering the application of EIA to the strategic level of policy making in the energy sector is establishing what constitutes that policy. The general difficulties in specifying and delimiting the object of policy analysis have been discussed in Chapter 2. Many academic and political commentators have made the point that the UK in the 1980s lacked an explicit energy policy, but that the government instead had 'a set of goals, policies and programmes which broadly defines the conventional wisdom in the field' (Owens, 1990). There were some challenges to this conventional wisdom. For instance, the inquiry into the Sizewell B PWR proposal included a debate on the government's energy policy, as part of the assessment of electricity generating strategies, but the departmental witnesses were unable to specify priorities among the objectives of establishing an energy market, and the need for diversity and security of supply (O'Riordan, Kemp and Purdue, 1988). External and international events, such as the Gulf War, as well as internal political priorities, such as reducing the public sector borrowing requirement, have continued to be major influences on the formulation of energy policy in the 1990s. The substantive elements of what Leach (1991) describes as the 'remnants' of government energy policy in the 1990s include strategies favouring energy conservation, the use of gas for power generation, and, to a lesser extent, the development of renewables, with some attention to the environment and Europe.

Government expenditure plans within the energy sector

Nevertheless, the government does set out its overt energy policy in a number of places. The report of the former Department of Energy on expenditure plans in the energy sector states the aims of UK energy policy as: 'to ensure that the UK has adequate, diverse, secure supplies of energy in the form that people and businesses want at the lowest realistic prices' (Department of Energy, 1992).

The report states that:

> The central thrust of the government's strategy is that the removal of obstacles to a more effective working of the energy market - particularly through the progressive dispersal of state control and encouragement of greater competition - offers the best and most efficient means of allocating energy resources to final consumers.
>
> Simultaneously, the government aims to maintain and promote the UK's wide diversity of energy resources, which is one of the key elements of security of supply. These aims are pursued within a regulatory framework designed to promote and foster the development of competition as well as protecting and advancing consumer interests. These various elements of policy are both complementary and mutually reinforcing. Better energy markets are creating greater diversity. Increased competition benefits and protects the consumer.

The report goes on to state that the (former) Department of Energy's detailed objectives are reviewed regularly, and points out that the current review has already given rise to a revised environmental objective, 'reflecting the increased importance of environmental issues in the Department's work'. These objectives are set out in Box 5.1.

The principal feature of these objectives is that there is no overt commitment to any particular energy source, nor any order of priority given to the objectives: so, for instance, the energy efficiency objective (5.) is given no particular weight. The consequences of this are discussed in Section 5.3.

Nevertheless, it is important to distinguish between the government's traditional policy objectives of security and diversity of supply, and their newer objectives of privatization and the encouragement of competition. The government has from time to time intervened in energy markets not only to secure diversified supplies of energy, but also to regulate to protect the consumer against monopolistic conditions, and to achieve environmental objectives. The principle of intervention is therefore clearly established. The question is whether these interventions reflect a consistent approach to the trade-off of these objectives against each other. One example can be seen in the way in which the regional electricity companies (RECs) were regulated on privatization to prevent the abuse of their monopoly. The terms of the regulation meant that 'in effect, RECs make more money the greater the volume of electricity distributed. Energy conservation and demand reduction are, as a result, highly damaging to their economic prospects' (Helm, 1991). Helm concludes that this intervention 'has been directly used to

---

Box 5.1 **Objectives of the Department of Energy**
(Department of Energy, 1992)

Within the framework of statute and of government policy, and having regard to international obligations and environmental implications, the central objective of the Department of Energy is to seek to ensure that the nation's needs for energy are met both now and in the future, whether from domestic or overseas sources, in the manner which makes the best use of both energy and other resources.

In particular, the department aims to further these objectives:

1. by discharging effectively and economically its responsibilities for licensing, regulation (including safety) and contingency planning in the energy field;
2. by promoting competition in energy matters;
3. by seeking to ensure that environmental aspects are properly recognized in all areas of the department's work; and that energy aspects are properly recognized in the development of the government's overall environmental policy;
4. through research and development (R&D);
5. through encouragement of efficiency in the supply and use of energy in the UK;
6. by maintaining, developing and implementing the appropriate framework of monitoring and control for publicly-owned bodies in the energy field, and transferring them to private ownership if and when this is desirable;
7. by ensuring a full and fair opportunity for the UK offshore supply industry to compete effectively at home and abroad;
8. by maintaining and developing an understanding of UK industries in the energy sector so that government policies and actions may, so far as possible, take appropriate account of their circumstances and contribute to their efficient development;
9. by maintaining and developing an understanding of the way energy is used in the economy;
10. by maintaining and developing public understanding of the role of energy in the economy and the policies and activities of government affecting the energy sector.

And, in pursuit of the above:

11. to manage the department's resources efficiently, economically and effectively.

---

pervert environmental objectives' (Helm, 1991). The case studies in this chapter elaborate on the way in which these conflicting objectives are pursued.

Moreover, in a partially privatized energy sector such as exists in the UK, it is important to distinguish between the government's stated energy policy, and the policies (for instance concerning market share, price, fuel substitution, and land assets) of the major corporate interests, both private and public. With the privatization of some industries in the energy sector, the interaction of their own objectives with those of the government and the regulatory agencies constitutes a key part of the way in which energy policy is implemented in practice. The importance of implementation of policy, particularly with respect to the evaluation of the outcomes of policy, has been emphasized in Chapter 2. For instance, the consequences in practice of the recent electricity privatization programme are only now beginning to be examined, for example by the House of Commons Energy Committee (HoC Energy Committee, 1992). It is not within the scope of this book to analyse these studies, but instead to draw out the many dimensions of policy formulation and implementation, and to highlight the question of the source and locus of energy policy, as a necessary preliminary step to considering the extent to which any requirement for SEA might be addressed.

The government's environmental strategy

The environmental objective of the former Department of Energy (item 3 in Box 5.1) referred to the interdependence of energy and environment, and it is clear that any review of energy policy needs also to examine that relationship. The government's environmental strategy as set out in the White Paper *This Common Inheritance* (SoS, 1990) required all Departments of State to produce a regular report on their environmental stewardship and objectives, which are included in various forms in the reports for the 1992 public expenditure round. For instance, the Department of Energy's Annual Report includes at Annex B a statement of its environmental objectives, activities and impacts. The White Paper also contains a number of statements of intent on energy, dispersed amongst various chapters, including that on Britain's Response to Global Warming. There is no single statement of energy policy in the strategy, but a number of commitments and targets (shown in Box 5.2). Although the White Paper was presented to Parliament jointly by the ministers for the key Departments of State, including energy, the fragmented attention to energy issues reinforces the view of UK energy policy as a set of disparate objectives and programmes.

The statements in the Annual Report and the White Paper need to be set alongside the government's electoral commitments, its day-to-day implementation of its objectives, and its responses to domestic and international issues. Central policies of the Conservative administration on the reduction of State intervention and on privatization of gas, electricity and (in prospect) coal have been significant determinants of energy policy. Other sources of policy lie in statements made in Parliament, in evidence submitted to Royal Commissions and Parliamentary Select Committees, and in the government responses to the reports of those bodies.

Box 5.2 Energy-related actions in *This Common Inheritance*
(SOS, 1990)
(numbers in parentheses denote chapters in the document)

- Help reduce Britain's contribution to global warming (5).

- Improve the efficiency with which energy is generated and used (5).

- Encourage the use of energy from renewable sources (5).

- Make people more aware of the environmental impact of their transport decisions (5).

- Improve vehicle fuel consumption (5).

- Encourage transport choice (5).

- At an international level reduce greenhouse gases, promote energy efficiency, reduce CO_2 emissions by the year 2005 to their 1990 levels, promote [combined heat and power schemes], set a figure for renewable electricity generating capacity under the Non Fossil Fuel Obligation, and encourage fuel economy and vehicle engine efficiency in the transport sector (5).

- Ensure that the planning system properly reflects environmental priorities through developing policy guidance on planning to conserve energy, such as guidance on development plan preparation and on planning and renewable energy (6).

- Reduce the levels of emissions from specific sources, such as vehicles, fuels and power stations (11).

- Full-scale review of nuclear policy in 1994 (15).

- Target research priorities on the development of cleaner technologies and more efficient use of energy, and encourage energy labelling of building products (17).

- Integrate environmental concerns into decision taking within government (18).

Government policy also manifests itself at the international level, in its support for and submissions to international institutions and conventions (such as the Intergovernmental Panel on Climate Change); in its dealings with the OECD (and the International Energy Agency (IEA), an autonomous body established within the OECD), the European Communities, and in political declarations of intent such as the European Energy Charter.

Existing scope for SEA

There are two points that can be addressed in discussing the application of EIA to the energy sector at a strategic level: whether a coherent and consistent energy policy is a prerequisite for SEA, and whether, in the absence of such a policy, SEA can make some compensation. Despite the government having an overt statement of policy, there are grounds for doubting that its constituent objectives are compatible, and therefore they may be inconsistently pursued. One of the advantages of a systematic approach to the appraisal of policy is that it enables these objectives to be clarified and given priority (DoE, 1991a). This section therefore examines the scope for SEA in the energy sector, while the next section looks at examples of plans and programmes within national energy policy.

Reference has already been made to the environmental objective of the former Department of Energy, whose 'central objective specifically recognizes that, in seeking to ensure that the nation's needs for energy are met, regard must be had to environmental implications' (Department of Energy, 1992).

However, the same report goes on to say that 'primary responsibility for managing and mitigating impacts from their own operations rests with the energy industries and users concerned. Government's role is to establish the appropriate framework for their environmental performance.'

This qualification neatly illustrates the difficulties in delimiting the boundaries of policy implementation in the energy sector. SEA as defined in Chapter 1 requires the formalized, systematic and comprehensive process of evaluating the environmental impacts of a policy, plan or programme and its alternatives, preparing a report on the findings, and using the findings in publicly accountable decision-making. Although the Secretary of State is given specific environmental responsibilities by statute in the regulation of the privatized energy industries, this does not constitute a formalized process of assessment; it does however give legitimate grounds for challenge and review. To be systematic would require the evaluation of alternatives and clear statements of objectives and trade-offs. It would also require the consideration of cumulative, secondary and indirect impacts, and local and global effects. The report of the former Department of Energy lists the possible array of impacts:

> No energy source is totally benign. All technologies for the production, conversion, transmission and utilization of energy have some impact on the environment, whether by consumption of natural resources, production of waste by-products, effects on landscape, or noise. These environmental effects can be diverse. Some are predominantly local in effect, others impact on national, regional and, in some cases, global levels of gases in the atmosphere (Department of Energy, 1992).

But this does not amount to guidance on assessing the impacts comprehensively.

There does not appear to be within the department any institutional mechanism for ensuring public, systematic appraisal of energy policies for their environmental effects. The White Paper on the Environment introduced the practice within Government of having a named minister within every department responsible for overseeing the environmental dimension. These 'green' ministers, as they are called in the First Year Report (SoS, 1991), 'stand accountable for the impact of all their Departments' programmes and policies', and the current crop of departmental expenditure reports incorporate annexes accounting for their actions in implementing the White Paper; but this in itself is not SEA.

Concern with the interaction of energy and environment is of course not new. A number of commissions of inquiry have been established, such as that set up by the Government in the late 1970s to advise it on the interaction between energy and the environment. This reported in 1981 on Coal and the Environment (Commission on Energy and the Environment, 1981), but the Commission was not reactivated in the 1980s. The Royal Commission on Environmental Pollution also undertook a comprehensive study of nuclear power and the environment (RCEP, 1976); the future role of the Commission has been under review, but its decision in 1992 to examine the environmental implications of the transport sector may herald a new phase of activity.

One area where there has been active assessment of the issue has been at the level of intergovernmental organizations such as the IEA. The IEA has identified major areas of environmental concern in energy production and use, and has examined the cost-effectiveness of adopting particular pollution control technologies or instruments (fiscal or regulatory) for reducing these impacts. The UK is a participating country in the IEA, but the terms of reference for the agency are essentially to provide an overview rather than to recommend particular strategies to member states. Nevertheless, some of their conclusions are material to SEA, and are discussed in the concluding section of this chapter.

At a domestic political level, the Parliamentary Select Committees have largely taken over the role of strategic overview. They have a formal status, and are empowered to examine the trade-offs between the different objectives of different Departments of State (and within departments) and, most importantly, to bring these into the arena of public debate.

The reports of the House of Commons Committee on Public Accounts on *National Energy Efficiency*, and that of the House of Lords Select Committee on the European Communities on *Energy and the Environment* (1991), are two recent examples of such attempts at systematic examination of energy issues. The House of Commons Energy Committee was empowered to review (and publish its findings on) the activities of the Department of Energy and its subsidiary public agencies, and, in the late 1980s, the interaction of public and privatised sectors. The value of the committee's activities has been described: 'they deal with economic, commercial and political aspects in a broad across the board perspective, and provide a reasonable summary of what is going on. If the Committee did not exist, something like it would have had to be created to take stock of the confused energy scene' (Bailey, 1991). With the incorporation of the former Department of Energy into the Department of Trade and Industry after the April 1992 General Election, the committee was disbanded. It is not yet clear where its responsibilities will lie in future.

The institutional scope for SEA of the overall energy sector in the UK therefore looks unpromising. Nevertheless, there are constituent plans and programmes within the sector where there may be more potential, and these are examined below.

5.3 Case studies of the energy sector

Case study of plans: energy in land-use planning

The land-use planning system in the UK involves a structure of policy from national planning policy guidance, regional guidance, and local development plans to development control, and recent legislation (regulations laid under the Planning and Compensation Act 1991) requires local authorities to take environmental considerations into account when preparing their development plans. These considerations include energy generation and energy conservation.

Energy conservation as such has not in the past been integrated into forward planning or development control in the UK (Owens, 1991), although energy policy and provision have had an effect on the land-use planning system at a general level (Cope, Hills and James, 1984). But in 1990 the government began to respond to a number of arguments that such integration was one way of meeting requirements for greater energy efficiency in the medium to long term (Warren, 1990). In the White Paper *This Common Inheritance*, the government confirmed that it had 'already asked Local Authorities to have particular regard to the conservation of energy as an issue in development plans' (SoS, 1990).

The most recent expression of this change of attitude has been in the final version of PPG12 (DoE, 1992a). The two principal references to energy in the PPG are in Section 5.9, indicating the key topics for which policies should be included in any structure plan or Unitary Development Plan (UDP) Part 1 as including 'energy generation, including renewable energy', and in Section 6.10–6.16 on 'energy conservation and global warming'. The emphasis in the latter section is on limiting emissions of greenhouse gases, whereas the draft version of the PPG had referred more broadly to the conservation of non-renewable resources such as land and energy.

The evidence assembled by Susan Owens in her report for the CPRE (Owens, 1991) was that:

although a substantial minority of planning authorities already make some explicit reference to energy efficiency in plans and policies, and many more intend to do so in future, there remains considerable confusion about the legitimacy of energy efficiency as a land-use planning issue. The strongly felt need for a statutory and policy framework was one of the most consistent findings to emerge from the [CPRE] survey.

The guidance given in PPG12 may be the beginning of that policy framework, but it is far from being fully developed, and is not mandatory. As the PPG says, 'the full extent to which land use planning can contribute to global environmental objectives has yet to be explored in sufficient detail to permit the government to offer definitive guidance'.

Nevertheless, for the principles in the PPG to be consistently applied, the environmental appraisal of the policies in the development plan should include a systematic consideration of the energy implications of the policies, in terms of energy generation and consumption. Although a number of plans do include policies to further such aims (such as Nottinghamshire and Cornwall's approved structure plans, Leicestershire's draft structure plan, and Sheffield's draft UDP), there is little evidence that any such appraisal of the energy implications of the plan or its other policies and proposals has taken place. This is not surprising, as there is little evidence of major projects being appraised for their energy implications (see section 5.4), and at the more complex level of land use plans the problems of understanding and prediction are magnified.

The government in PPG12 does, nevertheless, seem to have given support for some form of SEA in the development plan process. However, the principle has not extended to other government guidance, such as the PPG on Renewable Energy, available in draft form at the time of writing (DoE, 1992d), nor to the regional guidance issued by government. The draft PPG on Renewable Energy recognizes the need for some consideration of alternative sites and developments, but only in designated areas such as National Parks and Areas of Outstanding Natural Beauty, and within the context that in such areas the benefits of renewable energy may override the protection afforded by designation. English Nature recommended that the final PPG should encourage the inclusion of criteria-led indicative strategies in development plans to provide a framework for assessing renewable energy projects (English Nature, 1992), which would represent an opportunity for strategic assessment of their environmental implications.

The earlier crop of regional planning guidance issued by the government has not been subject to SEA for its energy implications, the final guidance for East Anglia making no reference to energy at all. Energy as such is being given attention in the South-West, North-East and East Midlands (Marshall, 1992), but references to more efficient production and reduction of consumption remain 'rather stranded from their housing, industrial and locational policies'. There are signs, however, that the later conferences on regional issues such as the West Midlands Regional Forum of Local Authorities (1991) may go further in examining the energy content and environmental implications of their strategies. These tentative steps do not satisfy all the criteria of SEA in being formalized, systematic, comprehensive or public, but they are moves in the right direction.

It is sometimes argued that energy planning for a region is an out-dated concept with demand being met by national companies, but evidence from the Continent shows that there is scope for effective and efficient regional energy planning (Nijkamp and Volwahsen, 1990; Bachtold, 1991; Barton, 1990). There is some experience of this in the UK at sub-regional level in Cornwall and Avon, and work has been done by the South-East Economic Development Strategy (SEEDS). The Cornwall Energy Project (Martin, 1990) assessed energy supply and use in that county, and examined energy conservation (Cornwall at that time importing almost all its energy). The project involved the mapping of sites for renewable energy initiatives against constraints (such as landscape designations), but did not amount to a strategic assessment. (Other studies of renewable energy are discussed below). Work is being done on simple predictions of energy use and emissions for Avon (Barton, 1991; Bristol Energy and Environment Plan, 1992), but both regional and sub-regional studies are hampered by the absence of baseline information on energy production and consumption at that scale, a necessary prerequisite for full SEA.

The Town and Country Planning Association's Working Group on Sustainable Development is suggesting that local energy strategies be drawn up by consortia of local government, business, voluntary organizations and area energy utilities (TCPA, 1992). This may overcome some of the problems of scant baseline information and could represent an opportunity for strategic assessment and integration with development plans.

In conclusion, it can be argued that the scope for SEA of energy in development planning is considerable:

> Energy is a fundamental resource, the use of which both influences and is influenced by the spatial structure of society. If planning is concerned with the use of land, then planners should be at least aware of the possible energy implications of their policies and decisions (Warren, 1990).

The government has accepted this position in PPG12, but needs to extend its expectation of what local planning authorities can do to its own national and regional planning guidance. It needs to encourage local planning authorities to include policies in their development plans requiring appropriate EIAs to include cumulative and secondary effects. It could also support the development of local or regional energy strategies with the necessary research to establish baseline data at that level.

Case study of programme area: energy efficiency

One example where it might be expected that the government would be undertaking a strategic appraisal of particular programmes is in its response to climate change and global warming. The former Department of

Energy's 1992 expenditure report states that 'the Environment White Paper identified energy efficiency improvements as the cheapest and quickest way of combatting global warming', which suggests that some form of strategic assessment had been undertaken. The report details the implementation of some of the measures promised in the White Paper, including the increase in the budget of the Energy Efficiency Office (since April 1992, part of the Department of the Environment). It lists the range of programmes, support and advice offered by the EEO to encourage the adoption of cost-effective energy efficiency measures, such as the expenditure on research and development including the best practice programme, and the targets for energy savings by the year 2000. Other programmes include those for home energy labelling, for support on the scheme on energy efficiency in low-income households, for a scheme for project management assistance with implementing energy efficiency measures, and major promotional, advertising and advice campaigns to corporate and householder consumers of energy.

The government asserted in the same report that a higher political profile was being given to energy conservation with the establishment of a Ministerial Committee on Energy Efficiency under the chairmanship of the then Secretary of State, and with an increased budget to the programme area. Nevertheless, the difficulties in reconciling competing political objectives remain. For instance, the government's own response to the report on energy and the environment by the House of Lords Select Committee states that:

> the Government believes that the economic case for energy efficiency is self-evident, and that there is good reason to promote it on a national level... there is an environmental imperative to improve energy efficiency throughout the EC (HM Government, 1991).

However, the Select Committee had commented that: 'there has been a slow-down in efficiency improvements caused by the recession and by "soft" energy prices', with which the government concurred:

> The financial incentive to invest in energy efficiency measures is affected by lower energy prices in that the cost-effectiveness of particular measures is reduced; the Government stated in the White Paper on the Environment that measures to stabilize CO_2 emissions at 1990 levels by 2005 would in the long term inevitably have to include increases in the relative price of energy (HM Government, 1991).

The former Department of Energy's 1992 report supports the committee's view in drawing attention to a short-term reversal in the trend of reducing national 'energy intensity' (the ratio of national energy consumption to GDP) in 1990, arguing that it was to a large degree caused by the recession and exacerbated by the reduction in energy prices (Department of Energy, 1992).

Such statements throw into question the government's overriding aim to secure energy supplies at the lowest realistic prices. This inconsistency between the objectives of the White Paper and the government's stated aim for energy suggests that, not surprisingly, systematic policy appraisal, highlighting conflicting objectives as would be required in SEA, is not being carried through.

This inconsistency is noted by the Energy Committee's report on the consequences of electricity privatization (HoC Energy Committee, 1992). The inquiry had strengthened their view that public electricity suppliers should be under a statutory obligation to promote more efficient electricity use, and the report concluded that 'the measures we regard as most important are amendments to the price control formulae to allow the cost of specific energy efficiency projects to be passed through and to remove incentives to sell more electricity'.

These views correspond with those propounded by the RSPB in its efforts to amend the Electricity Bill in the House of Lords, and reiterated in their evidence to the Energy Committee's Inquiry into Renewable Energy (RSPB, 1991b); these include giving the Secretary of State for Energy or the Director General of Electricity Services powers of veto, by allowing them to refuse or amend any application for tariff increase or major capital projects if public electricity suppliers had not shown satisfactory evidence of measures to promote energy efficiency.

This requirement would build a clear framework for comparison with alternative energy efficiency measures into the evaluation of applications to the Office of Electricity Regulation (OFFER) for authorization of capital projects for new generating capacity. It would enable the regulator to require that no new generating capacity should be installed until the potential for energy savings by that operator had been demonstrated as satisfactorily met. Given that one of the objectives of SEA is to consider alternatives before the commitment of capital expenditure, such an amendment to the regulator's powers would constitute an opportunity for the systematic appraisal of alternatives for their environmental effects. However, the 'environmental imperative' to improve energy efficiency would need to be explicitly built in as a presumption to such an appraisal.

Despite the move of the Energy Efficiency Office from the Department of Energy to the Department of the Environment, concerns may well remain about its budget (Association for the Conservation of Energy, 1992), and about the ability of the EEO to effect a change in the take-up of energy efficiency measures, particularly in the domestic sector. For instance, in November 1991 the government launched a voluntary retailer-led appliance labelling scheme with the co-operation of the regional electricity companies (RECs), but its implementation relies on the RECs, whose commitment may not be guaranteed. This illustrates well the problems described in Chapter 2 of the implementation gap, and the difficulties that this presents for the systematic appraisal of programme impacts.

Nevertheless, new opportunities are occurring for the more systematic integration of environmental considerations and energy programmes. One is the agreement by British Gas and OFGAS (the industry 'watchdog' body) for a new pricing formula allowing British Gas to pass through to its tariff customers costs associated with energy efficiency measures – the 'E' factor (Keay, 1991). OFFER has also issued a consultation paper on energy efficiency, including a discussion of least-cost planning, and a possible 'E' factor (OFFER, 1991); however it seems unlikely that under its present regime it will adopt either of these courses of action.

There is also some support in the business community for such measures. The report of the Advisory Committee for Business and the Environment (appointed by the Secretaries of State for Trade and Industry, and Environment), called upon the government to adopt a 'stronger position on the need for energy efficiency', and recommended changes in fiscal and regulatory policy to help reduce energy consumption (ACE, 1992).

The systematic appraisal of energy efficiency measures against their alternatives inevitably raises questions about the context in which those choices are made, including estimates of energy resources and requirements. Forecasts for energy supply and demand are problematic: for instance, the Department of Energy's projections for UK primary energy use in its submission to the IPCC (Department of Energy, 1990) have been criticized for their assumptions about price elasticities, trends and the possibilities for government intervention (Leach, 1991). The assumptions behind any revised projections need stating explicitly, in that they are likely to reflect the interpretation placed on the environmental imperative, and the extent to which it is regarded as a constraint. So, for instance, it would be theoretically possible to postulate environmentally sustainable amounts of energy production.

Inasmuch as these projections are seen as official or authorized by government, they represent one element in the government's overall energy policy, and as such could be subject to an SEA. But, as with the treatment of energy efficiency in the regulation of the privatized electricity industry, the application of SEA to these forecasts will not of itself guarantee greater weight being given to environmental considerations in trade-offs with other objectives. Even accepting environmental imperatives as over-riding would not avoid difficulties in defining an 'environmentally viable' level of energy production, as decisions would need to be made about the relative weights to be given to global, regional and local environmental impacts. These issues are discussed further below in the context of the justification for renewable energy and the appraisal of energy projects.

In conclusion, the extent to which it can be claimed that the government's commitment to energy efficiency is a result of any application of strategic assessment of the environmental implications of the programme is uncertain. Nevertheless, there is scope within the broad commitment of government for the central objective of environmental protection and the lower-order one of energy efficiency both to be given more weight. Such a systematic appraisal of the consequences of existing energy policy may be needed in order to meet obligations under the Convention on Climate Change agreed at UNCED in Brazil.

Case study of programme area: renewable energy

Another option that has recently found apparent favour with the UK government is renewable energy. The former Department of Energy's 1992 report devotes four pages to renewable and novel sources of energy, and a review of the 1988 strategy for renewables has been promised that will take account of the environmental costs and benefits of an enhanced programme (Department of Energy, 1992).

However, it is doubtful that this will examine the impacts of the broader framework within which renewables are promoted, such as the fiscal and regulatory regimes. For instance, the Non-Fossil Fuel Obligation (NFFO) and the Fossil Fuel Levy, imposed at the time of electricity privatization, imply a presumption in favour of projects for renewable energy by creating an initial market premium for renewables. The government's draft PPG on Renewable Energy (DoE, 1992d) reaffirms its policy 'to stimulate the exploitation and development of renewable energy sources wherever they have prospects of being economically attractive and environmentally acceptable'. However, concern has been expressed by conservation bodies (such as English Nature and the RSPB) who point out that current government policy in relation to the NFFO is stimulating exploitation of energy resources in just those areas where conflict with nature conservation is inevitable (English Nature, 1992). The draft PPG proposes a form of appraisal by planning authorities on a project-by-project basis, but a form of SEA instead would ensure the appraisal of the NFFO *itself* for its global and local impacts, and for its cumulative and indirect impacts.

Work on the possible environmental implications of the development of renewable sources of energy has been published (RSPB, 1991b; Ebrahimi and Elliott, 1992; Watt Committee, 1990a), but the regional studies by potential developers of the resource have a more limited scope. For instance, the NORWEB study of the North-West examined the prospects for energy generation from renewables mainly in terms of their technical feasibility, resource availability, and economic viability, examining the environmental implications of each technology on limited and non-standard criteria. Their review of landfill gas for energy generation refers only to the benefits in terms of managing the gas, and that for wave energy only refers to the visual effects. The report concludes that environmental effects 'need to be carefully evaluated for each project' (NORWEB/ETSU, 1989). The Department of Trade and Industry is now collaborating in further studies of the potential for renewables in the North-West, South-West, and Northern Ireland, and in county studies in Cumbria and Devon (*Review*, 1992). A consistent framework for those studies should include an appraisal of the potential in the context of the programme's fiscal and other support.

The role of the agencies responsible for renewable energy project appraisal needs explanation. Under the NFFO 'Will Secure Test', the former Department of Energy examined the technical and financial feasibility of schemes, and to some extent their likelihood in planning and environmental terms. The Renewable Energy Commercialization Section at the Energy Technology Support Unit (now part of the Department of Trade and Industry) gives advice on a project basis on EIA, and monitors the proposals in broad terms. It is therefore important that the department through ETSU is made aware of the cumulative and secondary impacts of such proposals (for instance, the impact of a series of offshore developments on the marine and coastal environment, or the necessity for lines to connect to the National Grid, or for sub-stations). These issues are discussed further in section 5.5.

In conclusion, the development of renewable sources of energy is still in its infancy, and this is a critical time for the development of good practice in establishing systematic appraisal of its effects. The agencies involved in appraising projects under NFFO need to ensure that they take consistent account of the full array of environmental effects.

Case study of programme area: orimulsion

So far, the policy and programme areas studied have been those with a substantial public or governmental input in terms of funding or fiscal regimes. But a critical feature of UK energy policy is the increased role of private sector activity following the privatization of fuel sectors such as gas, and of the electricity generation and supply industry. The case of orimulsion provides a good example of the scope for the application of an environmental appraisal at the strategic level to the fuel procurement policy of the privatized electricity generators.

Orimulsion is an emulsion of 70 per cent bitumen and 30 per cent water, using bitumen from the Orinoco Basin in Venezuela. As an emulsion, it flows more easily than the raw product, and can be transported more easily. It is being marketed in the UK by Bitor, a joint venture between BP and the Venezuelan State Oil Company. Both National Power and Power Gen have current proposals to burn orimulsion at oil-fired power plants, following initial trials.

Serious questions have been raised about the properties of orimulsion, and about the environmental effects of its combustion, in particular with respect to its sulphur content in comparison with heavy fuel oil or British coal. As was explained at the beginning of this chapter, the government's policy is to set a regulatory framework for the privatized electricity industry, but not to intervene within that framework. This framework includes targets for SO_2 and NO_x emissions to comply with the EC's Large Combustion Plants Directive. These targets are implemented through the UK Pollution Inspectorate (HMIP)'s authorization procedures for consent to discharge, and hence cascade down to the operators concerned. The government sees its role as marginal with respect to those agreed targets (although it would be involved in setting future targets), and as not being concerned with issues of the substitution of fuels within those targets.

Although BP-Bitor claim that a thorough assessment of the impacts of exploiting and using orimulsion has been carried out (Lewis, 1992), it seems that no strategic assessment is being undertaken by any UK regulatory agency of its environmental effects, or of the motives of the generators for turning to this fuel. The generators themselves argue that they need the fuel as it is cheap, plentiful, with stable prices pegged to those of international coal, enabling certain oil-fired plant to extend its economic life, and to reduce the need for older less efficient plant, while retaining the flexibility of the option of heavy fuel oil.

In this complex of commercial objectives (market share, fuel diversity, security), strategic assessment seems all the more justified. At present, it is being left to local planning authorities and to environmental pressure groups to point out the cumulative and secondary impacts of the development of orimulsion combustion capacity, both locally and regionally in terms of dust emissions, SO_2 deposition and acid rain, risks of fuel spills, and the environmental consequences of these. Other commentators have seen the broader implications of these proposals: the Coalfield Communities Campaign, for instance, links the shift to orimulsion with the shift towards the use of gas for electricity generation. The lower sulphur emissions of gas-fired plant enable the generators to keep within their sulphur emission targets, while burning cheaper orimulsion elsewhere (CCC, 1992).

In conclusion, the fuel procurement policies of the privatized generators have broader economic and environmental implications that need to be examined at a more strategic level than individual proposals. Assessments at the project level are discussed in the next section.

5.4 EIAs of energy related projects

Energy production

One way to evaluate the adequacy of existing EIAs of projects in the energy sector is to review the environmental impact statements (EISs) prepared. Projects can be seen as falling within particular stages of the fuel cycle or chain, from exploration, harvesting and processing, through transport, storage and marketing, to end use. Energy production projects are reviewed here in order of the first five of these stages.

As is shown in Appendix A.1, the EC Directive 85/337 requires that EISs be prepared (in the case of Annex II projects, depending on the significance of their effects) for:

- deep drillings (Annex II, 2.);

- extraction of coal, lignite, petroleum and natural gas (Annex II, 2.);

- briquetting of coal and lignite (Annex II, 3.);

- crude oil refineries (Annex I, 1.);

- installations for the gasification and liquefaction of coal or bituminous shale (Annex I, 1.);

- installations for the production, enrichment, reprocessing and storage of nuclear fuels and radioactive waste (Annex II, 3.);

- power stations of 300 MW or more (Annex I, 2.);

- nuclear power stations (Annex I, 2.);

- hydroelectric energy production (Annex II, 3.);

- installations for the production and/or transmission of electricity, steam and hot water (Annex II, 3.);

- overhead cables (Annex II, 2.);

- storage of gas and fossil fuels (Annex II, 3.);

- oil and gas pipeline installations (Annex II, 10.);

- installations for the storage and disposal of radioactive waste (Annex I, 3.).

A survey was undertaken of 59 EISs (those relating to energy production held in the Oxford Polytechnic collection of EISs), to make a preliminary assessment of whether the sum total of EISs would perform a similar function to that of an SEA for the energy sector.

The EISs were for the following types of development:

oil exploration (1)
opencast coal extraction (16)
gas/ethylene pipeline (4)
gas/ethylene terminal/processing plant (4)
power stations:
  combined cycle gas turbine (10)
  nuclear PWR (1)
  gas turbine (1)
  refuse/waste-derived fuel fired (2)
  combined heat and power (3)
  fluidized bed boiler (1)
windfarm (7)
incinerator producing energy as a side-product (3)
electrostatic precipitator (1)
transmission line (4)
gypsum disposal (1)

These were all the energy-related EISs held in Oxford Polytechnic's collection of EISs; as at early 1992, the collection comprised about one-third of the 700-800 EISs prepared in the UK since July 1988.

The EISs were reviewed to determine whether they addressed the following issues:

- need for the proposal;
- general explanation of proposal and site/process selection criteria;
- alternatives (location, process);
- cumulative impacts (of all current/proposed developments in a given area, of all developments in a given area over time, of all components of a given project).

These criteria reflect the issues that an SEA would be expected to address, but which individual project EISs would be less likely to address.

The large variety of types of proposals is noteworthy. Similarly, the types of developers preparing EISs varied enormously, from individual landholders hoping to diversify their activities (e.g. from farming to windpower) to major corporations with long histories of development (e.g. in the oil, gas and extraction industries).

Overall, the EISs were very good: using standard EIS review criteria (e.g. Lee and Colley, 1990), they would on average rank among the top one-quarter of EISs prepared to date. Nevertheless, the EISs reviewed generally did not address need, alternatives or cumulative impacts well.

Proposals for *opencast mines* generally explained the need for the proposal as relating to a statutory obligation to provide coal. Alternative sites and ways of removing the coal were not addressed at all: the proposed site can only be where coal is, and presumably other extraction methods would not be economically viable. More strikingly, all of the opencast proposals reviewed were on sites that had already been previously worked and/or were near extensive areas of existing or past opencast workings. However, the cumulative impacts of these developments were generally not discussed. In a few cases, the visual impacts of the multiple developments were noted, and one proposal referred to the historical geological disturbance. On the whole, however, the dearth of discussion of the cumulative impact of large areas of opencast mining was striking.

Pipelines and transmission lines were generally said to be needed because they connected with other proposed developments: power stations, oil platforms, gas processing facilities and the like. Thus, the EISs considered them as individual projects despite the fact that their *raison d'être* hinged on the approval and construction of another project. Alternative sites were generally well considered, since the major way of reducing their impacts (e.g. visual impacts for transmission lines) was to site them sensitively. Several EISs also considered alternative ways of achieving the same results. Only one EIS considered cumulative impacts: it discussed the total visual impact of several lines of transmission cables across a wide swathe of open land.

The EISs for the *gas terminals* scarcely addressed the need for the projects, but generally considered alternative sites well. One EIS addressed a range of alternative processes, particularly alternative uses for the CO_2 that the terminal would produce (e.g. in greenhouses). Again, the proposals were generally seen in isolation, without addressing transmission lines, pipelines or related projects. However, one EIS was quite different from the others. Although it did not discuss the need for the project, and although it disposed of alternative locations and processes in one sentence, it considered cumulative impacts well: existing and proposed nearby developments were described; the cumulative impacts of these developments on traffic, landscape, air quality and noise were addressed; and the conclusions again referred to cumulative impacts. The EIS also addressed the pipelines to and from the site.

Of the various forms of power station, *combined cycle gas turbine* (CCGT) stations were the most prevalent. They belong to the new generation of smaller, 'cleaner' but conventionally fuelled power stations; consequently, their need was justified by stressing the developers' obligation to fulfil the demands of the electricity distributors (who have a statutory duty to provide adequate supplies of electricity) and the CCGTs' cleanliness compared with coal- or oil-fired power stations.

Interestingly, the EISs for CCGTs considered neither alternatives nor cumulative impacts. Most of them mentioned greenhouse gases, usually by comparing the low level of such emissions from CCGTs with those from traditional power stations. Two nearly identical and nearly identically-timed proposals for CCGTs on adjacent pieces of land did not mention each other's potential impacts. Both EISs also mentioned that a third nearby parcel of land was being kept available for the construction of a very large (4000MW) fossil fuel-fired power plant, but otherwise did not refer to its potential impacts.

In contrast, the EIS for the *nuclear power station* did address alternative sites, and clearly assessed the cumulative impacts of other nearby power stations. Again, it justified need by stating the developer's statutory duty to provide electricity supplies.

The need for *other types of power station* was more clearly explained in their respective EISs. The two proposals for refuse-fired power stations referred to the need to reduce the volume of waste disposed of in landfills, whilst the EISs for the *combined heat and power stations* (CHPs) cited the need to provide cheap and clean heat and electricity. Consideration of alternatives was patchy, with better consideration of different locations than of different processes. None addressed cumulative impacts.

Various reasons were given for the need for the *windfarm* proposals, including the desirability of renewable energy. The general impacts of windfarms and criteria for siting them were explained well. Specific alternative sites were scarcely considered after general siting considerations were discussed. Alternative processes and cumulative impacts were not discussed at all; the areas where the windfarms were proposed are generally agricultural with few other existing developments in place.

The *incinerators which also generated power* were proposed primarily to dispose of wastes. The alternatives considered thus had to do with alternative forms of waste disposal rather than alternative ways of producing energy. None considered cumulative impacts.

The need for an *electrostatic precipitator* was given as being financial: the developer wanted to adapt the power station to burn orimulsion, but this would result in particulate emissions exceeding air quality standards, so an electrostatic precipitator was needed to reduce these emissions. The main alternative mentioned was the closure of the power station. The EIS did not address cumulative impacts.

An EIS for the *disposal of gypsum* produced as a side-product of a power station's flue gas desulphurization plant was particularly brief in terms of the criteria under discussion. It proposed no alternatives, did not discuss cumulative impacts, and noted only that the disposal site needed to be extended to accept the gypsum.

The survey revealed some important issues, especially in relation to the justification for schemes, an issue already raised in earlier sections of this book. First, EISs for less traditional forms of energy production (such as wind, or refuse-fired) generally emphasized the need for the proposal much more than those for more traditional forms (such as gas-fired or nuclear). This is despite the fact that the less traditional proposals are often less environmentally harmful in total than the more traditional proposals. The explanation lies in the fact that the cost of the energy generated, measured in price per kilowatt-hour, is probably higher than that for traditional means of generation, and therefore the projects need to justify themselves in terms of the environmental benefits they confer.

For conventional power stations, the statutory obligation to provide an adequate supply of energy was used as a major justification of need. In this light, it is understandable that the energy industry limits its scoping to alternative sites rather than alternative forms of generation. However, since privatization of the gas and electricity industries, the former Central Electricity Generating Board's obligation to supply has been removed. Moreover, 'there is already surplus generating capacity, so new stations can only be worthwhile if they produce cheaper electricity than existing stations and thus displace them, for example through fuel-substitution' (HoC Energy Committee, 1992). The justification for individual projects is therefore usually made in local terms of the replacement of capacity, leaving the wider issues of global impacts for government or international decision (Manning, 1991). In this context, the appraisal of the need for the schemes, and the alternatives, is rational and justifiable, but it is unlikely to emerge from the conventional project EIA process.

The consideration of alternative processes, for instance, might involve cross-national considerations. For example, the view has sometimes been expressed that the most cost-effective approach to achieving reductions in global warming might be by increasing energy efficiency in the formerly centrally-planned economies of Central and Eastern Europe (Watt Committee, 1990b), rather than by altering generation capacity in Western Europe. This raises major issues about the onus of responsibility on governments to take into account the regional or global implications of energy strategies.

A further feature of the reviewed EISs is a segmentation of projects, under which separate EISs had been written for each individual part. The justification for this was that different developers were responsible for different parts of the proposal, and that different applications were being prepared for different consenting authorities. For instance for one project, separate EISs were prepared for each of the different components of the overall scheme: a new natural gas pipeline from the North Sea, a gas reception and processing facility, and a CHP plant. Similarly, several EISs ignored other very similar proposals: for example two EISs for adjacent CCGTs made no reference to other proposed developments.

Finally, cumulative impacts were primarily discussed when a development was being built alongside, or to replace, an existing high polluter: for instance the CCGTs' emissions of greenhouse gases were discussed in relation to those of other types of power stations, and excavation and restoration of a previously abandoned mining area was proposed to improve amenities overall.

Energy use

Each of the stages in the fuel cycle described above may have implications for other stages which need to be considered: it is the thesis of this book that SEA would be one way to ensure that this vertical integration is achieved. The survey above shows that projects for energy production, while better than average according to the requirements of Directive 85/337, failed adequately to address alternatives, cumulative and secondary impacts, and other stages 'downstream' of the project. In taking a strategic view of the environmental impact of the energy supply chain in all its stages, the choice of alternatives and cumulative impacts of projects for the end-use of *consumption* also needs addressing. These end-uses can be considered according to sector of user (domestic, commercial, transport, iron and steel, industry and agriculture), or by functional use (space and water heating, other heating, cooking, lighting, transport, stationary motive power, appliances, and electro-chemistry and chemical feedstocks) (Reddish and Rand, 1991). These different end-uses do not correspond with the schedules of projects requiring EIA under the EC directive. An examination of the way in which EISs submitted under the regulations treat energy inputs and assess the impacts of that energy use will not, therefore, give a comprehensive review of these end-uses. Nevertheless, a review of a selection of EISs under the categories of project subject to the directive gives a broad indication.

The requirements of the directive, and the regulations which give it legal effect in the UK, are explained in a guide prepared by the Department of the Environment (DoE, 1989). None of the criteria given in the guide for identifying Schedule 2 (non-mandatory) projects relates directly to energy. The requirements of the regulations on the content of statements specify certain information for inclusion, including: 'the likely effects, direct and indirect, on the environment of the development, explained by reference to its possible impact on... material assets'. But the amplification of this specified information in the guide is not mandatory but discretionary: hence information on 'the nature and quantity of materials to be used', or the direct and indirect effects resulting from 'the use of natural resources', is not a formal requirement.

Elsewhere in the guide, other matters that *may* be included are listed. Energy matters come in this discretionary category, both in respect of information about the project and the assessment of the effects of the project.

A review of EISs aimed at examining the way in which they deal with energy therefore offers an indication of the interpretation of this guidance by both developers and competent authorities. In 1992, of the 182 EISs of energy-using developments held in the Oxford Polytechnic collection of EISs, three-quarters (134) made no mention of the project's demands for energy. Fewer than 20 per cent of statements mentioned the need for energy supply, and only a further 15 EISs estimated the amount of energy to be consumed (usually in the operation of the development rather than its construction). None of the road proposals estimated their energy implications. Little information was therefore being provided on the energy requirements of these projects, and certainly nothing on the effects of these energy inputs. The EIA process is therefore failing to consider some of the most important secondary or indirect environmental impacts of these projects.

Given the importance of energy inputs into so many human activities, some of which are covered by the EIA regulations, a major opportunity to review these inputs at a formative stage is being missed – this is particularly important in view of the government's commitment to energy conservation and efficiency. Such a review would not amount to requiring individual projects to justify themselves according to which uses less energy (it is accepted that this clearly depends on the type and technology base of the project, and rational economic interests would be expected to minimize energy costs), but would be more likely to bring out the full environmental impacts of the scheme. A role for SEA would be to undertake an assessment of the cumulative environmental consequences of energy use in branches or sectors of industry or economic activity, such as the transport sector, which has become the dominant consumer of energy and whose share is increasing.

5.5 The need for strategic environmental assessment

This chapter has to some extent taken for granted the importance of the energy sector in terms of its share of national economic output, its importance as an essential input to so many human activities, and its environmental importance. But the analysis has shown, through the case studies of plans, programmes and projects in the energy sector, that, despite the UK government's belief in decisions being made within a clearly laid out framework, trade-offs are being made (for instance between fuel economy and fuel security, between fuel resources and energy conservation, between environmental and economic and social goals) that are inconsistent with each other, and therefore presumably give the market conflicting signals. The operators in the energy market need frameworks to be consistent to enable their decisions to withstand future change, and are expressing concern at the lack of a strategic framework (Fells and Lucas, 1992).

One of the arguments for such a framework concerns the need for national guidance on global impacts and energy strategies generally, where the agenda is increasingly being set by international regulation and convention. For instance, the Effects Assessment Manager for National Power has argued that 'it is unrealistic to expect something as complex as a global warming analysis to be applied in the context of individual planning applications for combustion sources as this issue obviously requires national and international control.' He goes on to recommend that 'the application of [EIA] methodologies at national level to plans and policies should be the acknowledged way of dealing with the distributed and global effects of authorized power plant emissions' (Manning, 1991).

Although there may be problems in practice with the distinction between local, regional and global impacts, this recommendation deserves support. One model for such a framework for the energy industry may be the Netherlands 'Utilities Environmental Action Plan' (Lenstra, 1991).

Moreover, if further policy measures for environmental protection are to be introduced, the measures themselves will need appraising for their effectiveness. The OECD/IEA, for instance, has identified three areas for improved policy-making: the need to anticipate the macro-economic effects of such policy-instruments; the need for integrated analyses and responses; and the need for flexibility and effectiveness in environmental control (IEA, 1989). Such arguments have been repeated in more recent OECD work on the energy-environment interaction (OECD, 1991). The virtues of a more strategic approach are therefore being advocated by both governmental agencies and the energy industry, as well as by the conservation lobby.

This chapter has examined two issues in the application of SEA to the energy sector: (**1.**) whether a coherent and consistent energy policy is a prerequisite for SEA, or (**2.**) whether, in the absence of such a policy, SEA can make some compensation. It is concluded that, despite the evident difficulties in setting boundaries to energy systems in terms of their environmental effects, SEA would enable the fuller integration of energy objectives and environmental objectives, and hence assist in the development of a coherent energy strategy. The government could review with the industry and the competent authorities under the EIA Regulations and the Environmental Protection Act the need for guidance on issues of need, alternatives and the balance between local and global impacts. It could also ensure that the steps proposed in its own guidance on policy appraisal are implemented for framework-setting policies and for programmes such as energy efficiency. Such an appraisal will require further clarification of the government's broad environmental goals.

6:

Lowland heath

This chapter considers the use of SEA in taking a strategic view of the protection requirements of a particular restricted and vulnerable habitat system, lowland heath. It begins with a discussion of the importance of lowland heath and of the threats it faces. Existing EC, national and regional policies affecting lowland heath are reviewed. The lack of a national database and map of lowland heath distribution is highlighted as a major initial obstacle to any national strategic overview of the resource. Regional sources of information on heathland exist, but the information varies in form and quality. An analysis of EIAs prepared to date for projects affecting lowland heath shows that the potential impacts of these projects on heathland are not adequately covered, and that the application of project EIA does not inject into the decision-making process the right information to enable proper conservation of this fragile habitat. The chapter concludes with a discussion of the role of SEA in securing its protection.

6.1 The importance of lowland heath

There are three distinct types of heathland in the UK – maritime, upland and lowland heath – each of which exists under different climatic conditions and supports different communities of flora and fauna. Each is important in its own right. However lowland heathland can be regarded as particularly important both from a national and an international perspective, as 40 per cent of the world's distribution is found in the UK (Davies, 1989b).

Heathland in general is an important component of the British landscape. Heaths are not only visually attractive, but are also of considerable value as wildlife habitats. The flora and fauna have developed over 6000 years to give a unique ecosystem. Lowland heaths are the stronghold of rare animals such as the smooth snake and sand lizard, and birds such as the Dartford warbler. Other species such as the nightjar, hobby and silver-studded blue butterfly are only found locally in Britain but are well represented in this habitat.

Lowland heath was once found in large tracts in Cornwall, Dorset, Hampshire, Suffolk, Surrey and Sussex. However, changes in the use of land – particularly through afforestation and agricultural developments – have reduced its area at an alarming rate. Today lowland heaths remain at only a fraction of their original extent. Between 1830 and 1980 lowland heath in the areas mentioned fell from over 143,000 ha to 39,450 ha, a reduction of 72 per cent, the majority being lost between 1950 and the 1980s (Webb, 1986).

6.2 Threats to lowland heath

Historically, afforestation and conversion to improved farmland resulted in severe losses of heathland. More recently and notably in the Bournemouth/Poole conurbation (Dorset), urban development has also taken its toll. At present, one of the greatest threats to heathland comes from cumulative indirect impacts such as scrub encroachment, fragmentation and lack of management often associated with some form of development intention.

Forestry on lowland heath almost invariably involves the planting of alien conifers. Many areas have been lost to conifer plantations, such as Windsor Forest Heaths on the borders of Surrey and Berkshire. Once plantations become established, adjacent areas of heathland are in danger of being colonized by conifer seedlings. Encroachment is often unchecked as the timber is of economic value, whereas heathland is perceived as having no economic value. This self-seeding of conifers now forms one of the greatest threats to remaining heathland sites. In addition, most forestry management also requires the application of fertilizers to increase the nutrient level of the impoverished soils, and the drainage of wet heaths to make them more appropriate for tree planting, both of which are very detrimental to the heathland system.

Heathland is not currently directly threatened by loss to *agriculture* except in the most isolated of situations. However it is indirectly affected by nutrient enrichment from fertilizer run-off, which increases the rate of encroachment by scrub. Other agricultural practices such as the spraying of insecticides and herbicides may prove deleterious to heathland, as the spray may drift from agricultural land to adjacent heathland. Fragmented 'islands' of heathland surrounded by farmland are particularly vulnerable to this.

Heathlands are increasingly suffering from the encroachment of *urban development*, and many losses have occurred despite the designation of many such areas as Sites of Special Scientific Interest, National Nature Reserves, Local Nature Reserves, or Green Belt. Developments controlled by the planning process are frequently granted planning permission despite their impact on these areas. For example, much has been 'nibbled' away or fragmented to the extent that what remains is of reduced interest or viability, by the Department of Transport's road construction and improvement schemes: examples include the severance of Chobham Common by the M3 (the remainder now threatened again by the widening of this road) and Esher Common by the A3, and the quartering of Wilsey Common by the

A3-M25 interchange (NCC/SCC, 1988). The energy sector provides similar examples, such as the routing of pipelines. These may be directed through lowland heathland, often as a result of a lack of alternative land in highly built-up urban areas. Exploitation of another type of nationally scarce resource also threatens heathland; extraction of ball clay, which is found under Dorset Heath, may destroy the surface habitat.

Housing developments have resulted in direct loss to heathland as well as indirect losses due to degradation at the periphery of the site and opening up of access. Housing schemes that would damage heathland are still regularly proposed, despite a wider understanding of the problems.

Heathland is very sensitive and becomes rapidly degraded when subjected to excessive pressures from walkers, horse riders or motorcycle scramblers. The sharp increase in *tourism* in recent decades has placed increasing pressure on Britain's natural and scenic areas. Remaining areas of heathland have become subject to time-crowded and space-crowded impacts from recreational users.

Because heathlands owe their origins to past human activities, *management* is required to maintain their wildlife value. However the extent and effectiveness of positive management is limited by the costs of the labour-intensive work involved. Statutory site designation has not overcome this problem: in 1991 about 50 per cent of lowland heath SSSIs were said to be in need of better management (Rowell, 1991).

Finally, *fragmentation* is a major threat to lowland heath. Developments may reduce the size of individual blocks below that which is needed to keep them viable for many components of the community.

6.3 Policies regarding lowland heath

In recent years there has been greater official recognition of the importance of lowland heath. This section discusses relevant policies at international, national and county levels.

International obligations

In 1977 the Council of Europe adopted Resolution 77(5) on the Conservation and Management of Heathlands, which urged member states that still have heathland to recognize the habitat's uniqueness and cultural value, and to formulate policies to protect the remaining areas. It recommended that a European network of heathland Biogenetic Reserves be established, that fragments of heathland be protected by incorporating them into a national network of nature reserves, and that these protected areas be appropriately managed.

In 1979 the Council of Europe agreed the Convention on the Conservation of European Wildlife and Natural Habitats (the 'Berne Convention'), which seeks to conserve wild flora and fauna in their natural habitats. This protects, *inter alia*, certain listed species that are strongly associated with lowland heathland in Western Europe: the sand lizard, the smooth snake, hobby, nightjar, woodlark and Dartford warbler.

The 1979 EC Directive 79/409 on the Conservation of Wild Birds (the 'Birds Directive') places an obligation on member states to take measures to conserve the habitat of all wild birds, and to designate Special Protection Areas (SPAs) for the protection of listed species (including several heathland specialities) and other regularly occurring migratory wild birds.

UK government policies

Most heathlands are notified as Sites of Special Scientific Interest (SSSI). The Wildlife and Countryside Act of 1981, as amended in 1985, gave the Nature Conservancy Council (now English Nature (EN), Scottish Natural Heritage (SNH), and Countryside Council for Wales (CCW)) a duty to notify land that is of special interest by reason of any flora, fauna, geological or physiographical features, as SSSI. EN, SNH or CCW must provide the owners and occupiers of SSSIs with a list of Potentially Damaging Operations (PDOs); if the latter then intend to undertake any PDOs on the site, they must notify the statutory agency who have four months to respond. Notification as SSSI does not of itself fully safeguard habitats: for example, planning permission overrides the safeguards that the designation provides.

The fate of these sites is therefore often determined by decisions made at the discretion of local planning authorities who endeavour to 'balance' local development pressures against a stated national policy of safeguarding SSSIs (see for example, DoE Circular 27/87). Much therefore depends on interpretation of policy through guidance in, for example, circulars and PPGs, and through the development plan system (see below), rather than on legal prescription under wildlife legislation. Guidance must also reflect the tests that must be met by any decision to allow development which affects sites identified under international laws or conventions (such as those described above, and now including the EC 'Habitats' Directive 92/43).

DoE Circular 27/87 sets out, for example, the tests that must be met by such decisions where candidate or designated SPAs are concerned. A PPG on nature conservation (in draft at the time of writing: on publication it will replace the circular) does the same for Special Areas of Conservation under the Habitats Directive. Failure to follow this guidance could result in actions being brought in the European Court of Justice for alleged breach of one or other directive.

More generally, Circular 27/87 states that 'the Government wishes to ensure that its commitment to the achievement of economic growth without detriment to wildlife and natural beauty is fully reflected in local decision making' and 'the Secretaries of State wish to ensure that, as far as possible [SSSIs, NNRs, MNRs] are protected from damage or destruction, and their important scientific features are conserved by appropriate management'.

The SSSI status of a given area of land triggers certain other procedures intended to minimize the risk of local planning decisions undermining the national policy stated above. There are mandatory requirements under the General Development Order 1988 (as amended) for consultation between the relevant statutory conservation agency and the planning authority on planning applications affecting SSSIs. SSSI or internationally important status also affects the decision as to whether a project EIA is required under the EIA Regulations. Circular 1/92 (which is due later in 1992 to be subsumed into the new PPG) advises:

> consideration should be given to the need for EA where a Schedule 2 project is likely to have significant effects on the special character of an SSSI...The environmental effects of any proposed development either in or close to a declared or potential SPA or a Ramsar site should be subject to the most rigorous examination... In practice the likely environmental effects of Schedule 2 projects in declared and potential SPAs, Ramsar sites, and in declared NNRs and other sites identified under the Nature Conservation Review and Geological Conservation Review criteria will often be such as to require EA.

On occasion the 'balancing act' referred to above is too significant to be left to the local level, and the decision is 'called in' to be determined by the Secretary of State. Guidance on this is also given in Circular 1/92: 'The Secretary of State will normally call in planning applications – both within SSSI boundaries and outside – which are likely significantly to affect sites of international importance and recognized national importance.'

Notwithstanding these safeguards, much discretion remains with local planning authorities, and consent is often given for developments that are damaging to SSSIs. At national level, too, there are of course policies concerned with the promotion of development, and these are often allowed to override conservation policy, to the extent that questions of compliance with international conservation obligations are raised from time to time by NGOs and the European Commission. Developments controlled by the planning system are one of the commonest types of causes of damage to SSSIs (Rowell, 1991).

County policies

The statutory strategic development plans produced by county councils (structure plans) guide the broad location of future developments, and also express policy intent with regard to the safeguard of nature conservation interests, usually with specific reference *inter alia* to SSSIs.

Some county structure plans make particular provision for the protection of heathland. A review for the purpose of this book of 14 structure plans from the main heathland-rich areas of England showed that six (Berkshire,

Cornwall, Dorset (2), Norfolk and Suffolk) had specific policies for lowland heath. Norfolk's, for instance, states:

> County and district councils will, through development control and positive action, protect wildlife in areas of important wildlife quality, and in the following habitats: river flood plain marshes, rivers and streams, ancient woodlands, heathlands, areas rich in botanical species such as meadows, verges and former railway land, and other areas where rare species are known to be present. In areas without statutory protection, or where development which might threaten wildlife is not subject to planning control, the County Council will seek to protect important wildlife habitats by establishing Local Nature Reserves and entering into management agreements (Norfolk CC, 1990).

Four other structure plans (Devon, Surrey, Staffordshire and West Sussex) addressed heath in the course of more general policies, or otherwise mentioned the need to protect it. Devon's is an example:

> The County contains important wildlife habitats in both its rural and urban areas. Woodlands, hedgerows, unimproved grassland, heathland, ... are all important wildlife habitats. The retention of these and all other semi-natural habitats will be supported by the County Council, and encouragement will be given to landowners and managers to take advantage of financial assistance, available from various sources, for conservation work (Devon CC, 1991).

Four structure plans covering relevant areas (Hampshire (2), Kent and East Sussex) failed to mention heathland altogether.

In addition, various county councils and others organized on a county basis have drawn up non-statutory strategies concerning heathland. These include Dorset Heathland Forum (1990); Hampshire County Council (1984, 1989); Nottinghamshire County Council (undated); Staffordshire County Council/NCC (1989); Staffordshire Wildlife Trust et al. (1991); and Surrey County Council/NCC (1988). In Staffordshire a heathland project officer has been appointed by English Nature, and steps are being taken to establish a heathland forum.

Sources of data

Given that lowland heath is internationally rare and of concern to conservation bodies and planning authorities alike, one would expect a comprehensive database on the resource, including for example large-scale maps showing its distribution throughout the UK. However, this is not the case.

Most existing information on lowland heaths is collated on a county basis. Various environmental NGOs, such as the county wildlife trusts, hold some excellent information. However, obtaining any on a national basis for heathland is difficult and time consuming. Many organizations assume that 'someone else' has the full picture. Owing to the absence of a national database on lowland heathland it is difficult to analyse it at present in any other context than the regional or sub-regional.

No national map detailing the distribution of all lowland heathland in the UK appears to exist. Maps are available at a county level, primarily from environmental NGOs in those counties with significant amounts of heathland. For instance Bedfordshire has good 1:10,000 maps of its heathland; Cornwall Wildlife Trust has approximately 300 very good 1:10,000 Ordnance Survey maps of lowland heathland, but no summary map of the county; and Devon Wildlife Trust has a very basic map of lowland heathland in the county broken into $10km^2$ areas. Kent County Council designated a 58 ha heathland a Local Nature Reserve, but a county habitat survey has not been undertaken so it is not certain whether this is the full extent of heathland in the county. English Nature is currently collating information for lowland heath distribution via a 'Phase 1' habitat classification survey, but this is not yet complete. The RSPB is also collating distribution data on a more comprehensive basis.

6.4 EIAs of projects affecting lowland heath

Of 253 environmental impact statements prepared in the UK between 1988 and early 1992, nine (4 per cent) were for proposed developments that would affect lowland heath. Table 6.1 summarizes the results of a review of these statements in respect of their treatment of potential impacts on this habitat. The relatively low number of EIA cases affecting lowland heath may reflect the success of conservation campaigns in respect of this habitat in deterring intending developers at the outset.

Table 6.1 **Summary of EIAs regarding lowland heath**

Type of development	Number of ESs	County	Status of site
Road/rail	4	Dorset	SSSI
		Surrey	SSSI
		Bedford	undesignated
		Kent	SSSI
Energy	2	Bedford	SSSI
		Cornwall	SSSI
Extraction	1	Staffordshire	undesignated
Recreation	1	Devon	undesignated
Mixed-use	1	Kent	undesignated

The types of developments that were described in the statements are consistent with the types of development pressures discussed earlier. Six proposals were for road, rail or energy developments that were of more than local significance and might be regarded by their proponents as being of national importance.

The quality of the statements was generally average, compared with the quality of environmental statements overall (see Chapter 1). However, their discussion of impacts on the heathland was generally poor, and very few gave even basic details such as the area of heathland affected by the development. Of the nine proposed developments, five were related to SSSIs and four to undesignated sites, reinforcing the point made above that statutory designation gives no guarantee of protection.

6.5 Application of strategic environmental assessment

Generally, these days, lowland heath is well recognized as a valuable wildlife habitat, and receives a good degree of protection from deliberate destruction. In notified SSSIs few direct threats remain, although such sites are far from immune. Problems still exist at undesignated sites and in the smaller fragmented 'outliers', which are particularly vulnerable. All heathland sites, even those apparently protected, are vulnerable to indirect, cumulative or time and space-crowded impacts.

Given the importance of lowland heath, its limited extent and the pressures that are being exerted upon it, it could be argued that any strategic-level environmental assessment process should view this habitat in its entirety. Some form of strategic plan for the long-term future of the nation's heathland would help to facilitate this.

One prerequisite, which surprisingly appears not yet to be in place, would be a detailed database and map of the total resource. Without this information it will be difficult to view the resource as a whole and make decisions regarding its future. Ownership is one of the issues that this would need to address. Major owners of heathland include the Ministry of Defence, the Forestry Commission, the extractive and waste disposal industries (particularly sand and gravel industries and British Gas), local authorities, national and local conservation bodies, and the Commons Management Associations.

Some goals need to be established for the future management of heathland. Background objectives would include the conservation of all existing areas of lowland heath and an expansion and amalgamation of smaller fragmented 'islands'.

Measures to achieve these goals could include: a moratorium on development in certain sites; guidelines for activities that may have a detrimental effect on heathland (e.g. fertilizer use); and a strengthening of SSSI controls. The effectiveness of these measures would need to be monitored and adjusted as necessary.

The measures outlined above are not equivalent to SEA. While environmental evaluation of, for instance, development plans (see section on

PPG12 in Chapter 3) would offer much to heathland protection as well as to other habitats, the conclusion of this review is that it is less appropriate to organize a system of SEA according to one particular habitat, than by impacting developments, either sectorally or by geographical area. SEA of sectoral PPPs affecting lowland heath (e.g. the extractive industry, housing and other forms of urban development, amenity-related activities and road building/widening), would be able to cater for the strategic planning of heathland if set against the national strategy described above, and coupled with proactive management measures.

Sectoral or area plan-based SEAs would need to identify the range and importance of the habitat and the interest groups involved. An umbrella group could be set up to advise and co-ordinate activities affecting the habitat, to set objectives, and draw up a management strategy. SEA, while thus not being organized primarily around a strategy for the conservation of individual habitat types, would nevertheless provide ways of enhancing the means by which their strategic conservation needs were met.

7:

Strategic environmental assessment and global futures

Much of this book has concerned the extension of EIA from the project level to more strategic levels. This chapter proposes a much greater role for SEA in contributing to a framework for the achievement of environmental sustainability. It attempts to define sustainability and to clarify the links between SEA and sustainability. If sustainability is put forward as the overriding objective for SEA, then a much more powerful and demanding system of SEA can be developed, which will ultimately improve existing environmental conditions and predict and mitigate against future ones. However, this chapter also shows that the concept of sustainability and its implementation in practice is problematic. The proposals put forward in this chapter are by necessity broad-brush, and would need to be supported by many more specific initiatives before they could be implemented.

7.1 A sustainability-led approach to strategic environmental assessment

The environment and economic development are inextricably linked. This was shown 20 years ago in the Club of Rome study (Meadows et al., 1972), and has been repeated in subsequent studies, including those preceding the recent Earth Summit in Rio de Janeiro (see Box 1.2). In these 20 years, methods for environmental analysis have progressed and become widely accepted, but the problems involved in reconciling the often conflicting needs of conservation and economic development have in many cases become worse (see, for example OECD, 1991; UNEP, 1989; WCED, 1987). Industrial concerns in developed countries argue that many environmental measures are at best misguided and at worst subversive to our way of life. Similarly, developing countries are loath to accept any forms of control over the (often unsustainable) use of their resources.

However, a major advance of environmental policy in the last 20 years has been the growing acceptance of the need to use and manage the world's resources in a way that is sustainable. *Environmental sustainability* has many definitions, but they all include the notion of the continuity of a resource base over time. For instance, Jacobs (1991), defines sustainability as meaning:

that the environment should be protected in such a condition and to such a degree that environmental capacities (the ability of the environment to perform its various functions) are maintained over time: at least at levels sufficient to avoid future catastrophe, and at most at levels which give future generations the opportunity to enjoy an equal measure of environmental consumption (Jacobs, 1991).

Gow (1992) notes that sustainability should mean that the local population does not degrade its natural resource base, or at least not irretrievably, but rather that it should conserve or improve its natural resources. He goes on to say that 'development', in contrast, demands that human life somehow improves.

Gow's distinction between the goals of sustainability and of development is challenged by the more widely accepted concept of *sustainable development*. The definition of sustainable development given by the Brundtland Commission (WCED, 1987), which appears regularly throughout the literature and is well accepted, is 'development which meets the needs of the present without compromising the ability of future of generations to achieve their needs and aspirations'. The Brundtland Commission claimed that human poverty is a major cause of environmental degradation, and that a goal of sustainable development should be 'meeting the basic needs of all and extending to all the opportunity to satisfy their aspirations for a better life'. Similarly, Stedman and Hill (1992) suggest that sustainable development is fundamentally about human well-being: about human dependence on natural resources and the almost universal desire for economic improvement.

This highlights a major distinction between the concepts of sustainable development and sustainability, namely the question of whether sustainability and development can go hand in hand or not. Sustainable development assumes that they can; sustainability does not make that assumption. The concept of sustainable development is promoted by parts of both the development industries and the 'green' movement, primarily because it appears to provide the best of both worlds. However, if development and sustainability are not compatible, it is doubtful that sustainability will be embraced as wholeheartedly as sustainable development is. The principle of sustainability is advocated here over that of sustainable development for reasons of 'precaution': lack of information about any topic should indicate that no assumptions can be made within it about the compatibility of sustainability and development. Sustainability can encompass sustainable development, but the reverse does not hold true.

The concept of sustainability (or sustainable development) can be made operational in the form of *carrying capacities*. Carrying capacity is a function of a number of variables:

- the region in question, e.g. a watershed, the world;

- the type of resource in question, eg. water, energy, whatever resource would limit the growth of the human population;

- what is being 'carried', e.g. human population, noxious gas emissions;

- whether the resource is assumed to be constant or is changing over time, and whether it is renewable or not;

- whether what is being 'carried' is assumed to be constant or not;

- value judgements, e.g. ideal/optimum capacity versus maximum/minimum capacity.

In order to ensure sustainability, carrying capacities should not be exceeded. In the past, development has taken place on habitat types, which, once removed or disturbed, cannot be regained: Box 7.1 gives an example of this. Heathlands, discussed in Chapter 6, are another example.

Box 7.1 Destruction of an irrecoverable habitat: afforestation on Scottish peat bogs

The huge afforestation programme that has taken place on the peat bogs of Caithness and Sutherland in the north of Scotland is an example of the destruction of an irrecoverable habitat. The blanket bogs of Caithness and Sutherland are comparable to a tract of rainforest in that they are of global significance owing to their unique ecosystem. This area of peat is the largest single area of habitat in the United Kingdom that is of major importance on the world scale because of its global scarcity (NCC, 1987b).

The significance of many of the plantation schemes on these peat bogs is individually minimal in such a vast area. However, by 1987 at least 79,350 ha had been planted or were programmed for planting, 67,000 ha of which were on peat. If, via the SEA process, the afforestation programme had been looked at in its entirety before any planting took place, then this large-scale destruction of what is arguably the UK's most important habitat type might have been avoided.

To ensure that carrying capacity is not exceeded, the current state of the resource and its uses must be monitored; predictions must be made concerning the future state of the resource and its uses, and the possible use of alternatives; and mitigation measures must be made available to be implemented if the uses exceed, or threaten to exceed, the carrying capacity. This is *strategic environmental assessment*. In turn, SEA requires information about the environmental impacts of specific projects. Finally, additional monitoring is needed to ensure that all these steps are carried out correctly.

This suggests that sustainability could be achieved through the following sequence of steps:

- a global commitment to the objective of sustainability;

- a determination of the parameters within which sustainability is to be achieved, i.e. area, resource, use, time and expected 'level' of sustainability;

- a determination of carrying capacity based on the above. This determination would also aim to achieve international development targets, e.g. for CO_2 emissions. An example of such a study is the Netherlands' 'Concern for Tomorrow', which has determined that many forms of emissions would need to be decreased by 70 to 90 per cent to be sustainable;

- SEA of all PPPs affecting the environment; this could take the form of sectoral and/or regional SEAs. These should be superimposed over habitat-based management plans; appropriate alternative development scenarios would be produced, which fulfil the criterion of not exceeding the region's carrying capacity; one of these would then be chosen to optimize political and socio-economic factors (the important thing is that these two steps are conducted in this sequence, not the reverse as is currently more frequent). Various scenarios of increased or decreased consumption or production could be tested (by running theoretical models, or in practice) to determine whether they would maintain the carrying capacity;

- environmental impact assessment of individual projects within the constraints set by SEA (such that project EA becomes a 'second tier' within the framework of the first strategic tier);

- a monitoring programme to give feedback that would allow any/all of the above to be adjusted. For instance, monitoring would identify ecological resources and functions in danger of non-sustainable use, providing triggers for action and a basis for initiatives to restore sustainability. It would also enable a set of ecological accounts to be drawn up, allowing a 'balance of trade' between region and biosphere to be determined.

The central feature of this system of SEA is the way it allows the principle of sustainability to be carried down from policies to individual projects and beyond. It allows SEA to be viewed as an integral step in the attainment of sustainability. It sets the theoretical requirements of sustainability in a practical context, and establishes a framework within which project EIAs can be carried out.

This is a considerably broader, and more impressive, role for SEA than the limited one generally considered so far. The 'incremental' approach discussed earlier in this book aims slowly to broaden the remit of EIA 'upwards' from projects to programmes, then plans, then policies; it aims to achieve sustainability by a form of grassroots incrementalism.

A major role for SEA must be to move beyond a sectoral approach, to look at ways in which development decisions can not only prevent environmental harm but positively enhance natural resources. SEA could emphasize the need for a more integrated approach to potential land use strategies that looks at the land resource in terms of productivity, stability and sustainability. It could also help to determine the best combinations of land use, while accounting for the properties of the natural resource base. However, this will only occur if environmental factors are given adequate consideration at the earliest stages of formulating development objectives. SEA potentially has a major role in encouraging this consideration in PPPs and moving away from short-term approaches, which inevitably result in the non-sustainable exploitation of natural resources.

7.2 Issues and problems with the sustainability-led approach to strategic environmental assessment

Unfortunately, the general acceptance of the principles of sustainability and carrying capacity has not been matched by understanding of the mechanisms involved. Sustainability, carrying capacity, and their translation into objectives for SEA have many theoretical and practical problems, over and above the institutional ones of setting up a system of SEA.

An initial problem with the various definitions of sustainability is that they are very broad based, engendering scepticism about their ability to be implemented. This is illustrated by Gow (1992) who asserts that 'sustainability is like happiness – everyone believes in it and everyone has a different definition'. He adds that 'sustainability has become so all-encompassing as to be virtually toothless, whether it is financial, institutional, economic, environmental, or technical, to name a few of the more common manifestations'.

As was discussed in chapter 2, many countries have rigid institutional systems lacking the flexibility required to achieve precautionary, long-range objectives such as sustainability. Government agencies often have a very compartmentalized definition of their activities, which limits their ability to achieve broad strategic goals. National policy does not always lend itself to formal rigorous appraisal for substantive areas (those giving direct rise to physical developments) or for cross-sectoral areas such as fiscal and budgetary policy. The policy may not be explicitly stated, or it may be subject to continuous interpretation and adjustment through the normal political process of government. The ideal of a coherent and consistent overall policy, from which flow environmentally benign plans, programmes and projects, does not reflect political realities. The lack of available and reliable information exacerbates this situation.

The Australian government's goal of 'ecologically sustainable development' (ESD), which they aim to achieve via major legislative reform at the national and state levels (Sandford, 1992), is commendable in this respect, although the actual implementation of ESD is likely to be a complex and lengthy matter:

'To achieve the transition to ESD, Australia needs policies, structures, and processes that can deal in prospect rather than in retrospect, that can take full account of the social, economic, environmental, cultural and political realities of a rapidly changing world, and that have the capacity and flexibility to manage and resolve cross and intersectoral environmental and resource use conflicts.

The concept of *carrying capacity* is also problematic. A calculation of carrying capacity requires an understanding of how much of the resource is available. From an ecological perspective this is often difficult: for many areas the information base is at best incomplete and at worst non-existent (see, for instance, chapter 6). In addition, attempts at measuring carrying capabilities conducted at single points in time will tend to be self-defining: i.e. what is seen to be 'sustained' at that time is taken to be at or below the capacity, whereas it may be *unsustainable* over a *period* of time. The ecosystems to which SEA would be applied are often complex and unpredictable, and in many case studies even the definition and delimitation of habitat types can be disputed. The Biodiversity Convention of 1992 may be a step towards rectifying this situation: as Pearce (1992) points out, the treaty has moved beyond only preserving wild areas with exceptional diversity to encouraging the 'sustainable development of biological resources' (but see earlier comments on the distinction between 'sustainable development' and 'sustainability'). Other similar moves may assist in the application of SEA, as they would provide much-needed information on which to base global environmental decisions.

As was previously mentioned, carrying capacity is linked to definitions of area, time and resources; different carrying capacities are interlinked; and outside factors such as technological innovation affect carrying capacity. The models of carrying capacity developed to date by necessity tend to consider regions as self-contained and closed. However, in reality regions are not closed, and the carrying capacity of one region is affected by that of another. For instance inter-regional trade has allowed the carrying capacity of one region to be exceeded by depleting the carrying capacity of another (Rees, 1988). These factors also affect the use of SEA since the definition of boundaries for the relevant policy, plan or programme is a necessary step in SEA (see Appendix C).

Other problems exist. The types and uses of various resources are not well known. For instance, differences around the world in per capita resource consumption will affect carrying capacity: the planet can accommodate more people with low resource requirements than those people with high resource requirements. Technological innovations can have major impacts (both positive and negative) on carrying capacity, while in general technology has allowed humans to wreak environmental havoc far beyond their own physical power. Carrying capacity also relies on inherent value judgements, and on the use of non-biological standards against which the severity of an impact can be measured. Research into the field is in its early days and until the concept is more widely accepted and well-developed, studies on carrying capacity are likely to be expensive and protracted.

The *value of resources*, and the extent to which they can be traded against each other, has been the focus of much recent research and debate (e.g. DoE, 1991a; Pearce et al., 1989). The most pressing issue related to this topic is that of matching natural resource capability to the needs of society; past lack of consideration of this problem has resulted in large-scale habitat destruction, over-exploitation of natural food stocks (sometimes resulting in extinction), and unacceptable levels of a range of emissions. Methods of assigning values to natural resources must be also devised and agreed on: many attempts have been made to try to assign values to natural resources (e.g. Pearce et al., 1989), none of which are ideal.

Another issue is that of potential capability versus existing capability – just how much pressure can natural resources withstand before they collapse completely? This question will probably never be fully resolved, as what is seen by some as under-utilization will be seen as over-utilization by others. However, SEA could provide an overall picture of the current state of the resource, indicate the maximum amount of use, and provide a systematic approach that allows the major components of impacts on a global scale to be identified. Crucially, it would provide a consistent framework within which to make the necessary value-judgements, on an accountable basis.

Problems also arise concerning the *trade* (in the broadest sense) *in resources*. One issue is whether all global resources should in theory be tradeable, or whether certain resources are so fragile that no trade of any description should take place (i.e. they are 'priceless'). Decisions concerning levels of fragility (and therefore the point at which trade is no longer acceptable) are very contentious. Another issue is how the needs of 'the environment' are to be balanced against those of people: in many cases indigenous peoples need to over-exploit globally declining and 'fragile' resources simply to stay alive.

Given these problems, it is understandable that, although some theoretical literature exists on the need for strategic environmental assessment, the practice of SEA has been much more limited (see chapter 3). Experience outside the UK has been largely confined to programmes and development plans, and not based at the level of national policy-making. SEA systems are also generally still new: examples of the way in which SEA has actually improved the decision-making process, or has been incorporated into that process, or shown tangible benefits for the environment are still rare, making conclusions uncertain.

There are also objectives that SEA will not of itself fulfil. These include giving greater weight to the environment; giving increased protection to, for instance, SSSIs or Special Protection Areas; and treating the environment as an overriding constraint. The sum total of all sector-based SEAs is unlikely to give the same amount of environmental protection to an area as a regional SEA. Some sectors are unlikely ever to be subject to an SEA, either because they are too small or because they are too sensitive: thus the impact of these sectors would not be considered. The negotiations surrounding the agreement on constraints set by carrying capacities are also likely to be extremely long and complex. On the other hand, region-based SEA has problems as well: links between regions have to be forged (like those between sectors), not all impacts in a region can be predicted, and flows between regions make it difficult to predict carrying capacity adequately.

Perhaps the most intransigent problem, however, is that the concept of sustainability-led SEA is not yet a politically accepted one. The current economic climate, the UK's traditional incremental approach to policy making, the worldwide emphasis on economic well-being (e.g. GNP) rather than total quality of life, and the sheer effort involved in determining criteria suitable for sustainability, all frustrate the concept of sustainability-led SEA on the grander scale described above.

7.3 Strategic environmental assessment in the future

Despite its problems, sustainability provides a focus and objective for SEA. The need to limit environmental impacts for the sake of human survival is inherent in the concept of EIA. There must be a move away from the present development-centred approach to land use, to one which has environmental sustainability as a prime objective; SEA provides the most comprehensive approach to doing so.

In an ideal world *SEA should be based on sustainability*, and in turn it would cascade this down to project planning. Sustainability should be based on carrying capacities, which then set environmental thresholds that are not to be exceeded. *Within* these constraints, other factors (social, economic) can be optimized. However, in our less than ideal world, changes take place incrementally: SEA at present is coming about as an application of a known technique to a slightly higher level of decision making. This real life incremental view limits the 'strength' and theoretical elegance of SEA: however, the incremental approach may often be the best way forward.

In all probability the best approach will be to *combine the ideal theoretical system with the incremental real-life approach*. Governments should fund further research into sustainable development, carrying capacity and SEA at the highest policy levels, while at the same time carrying out incremental changes to their existing systems of EIA.

In order to implement a sustainability-based system of SEA *governments should commit themselves to sustainability* and to making it an objective for all of their PPPs. The limitations of studies regarding sustainability and carrying capacities should not prevent the use of these concepts, nor further research into their increased application. The goal of early studies should not be to identify a precise figure for energy consumption or levels of emission for instance, but rather to give an indication of the directions and magnitude of change needed. The Netherlands' study on carrying capacity, with its broad mandate to reduce emissions by 70 to 90 per cent, breaks new ground, not necessarily (or solely) for its scientific vigour, but because it gives an idea of the magnitude and direction of the changes that must be made to achieve sustainability. Similar studies should be carried out both in developed and developing countries, and their findings implemented. Once this has been achieved, more detailed studies will need to be carried out in order to refine the concept, and to make any necessary changes. Governments should also commission studies on carrying capacities for various sub-regions as well as for their countries as a whole. These studies should propose broad limits for various forms of resource use and/or types of development.

The framework within which such decisions are taken is all-important. SEA can greatly assist by building a system of weighting into the formal appraisal process that will give overriding, and in some cases infinite, weight to environmental constraints. Carrying capacity studies will assist with this process. However, this will not be easy to achieve as there will be many instances where global benefits clash with the immediate needs of local communities. The SEA framework must take this into account – the emphasis cannot be only on the natural environment.

By *adopting the precautionary principle*, this information could be acted upon now, while additional more precise data are collected for an improved round of calculations. Changes could then begin to be made before environmental conditions deteriorate further, removing the 'bolt-on' approach to EIA that is particularly prevalent under the current systems. Any changes are likely to be difficult as their instigators are likely to be accused of having ulterior motives, failing to be realistic in what they ask for, or demonstrating a lack of political awareness.

Although the various SEA systems established by individual countries have had varying degrees of success, they are exactly that – individual attempts. Not all impacts in a country can be predicted, and flows between countries make it very difficult to predict carrying capacity adequately. *Countries must work together* to look at the potential cumulative impacts of their activities and SEA provides an ideal framework with which to do so. Only if every country gives adequate consideration to its environmental resources when formulating its PPPs can the globe's environmental wealth be maintained.

Global SEA would require governments to carry out several steps. First, they should initiate programmes that estimate carrying capacities and associated targets for all those areas currently associated with 'global' problems. Second, they should commission studies into carrying capacities in the context of sustainability. Third, SEA should be required as a formal procedure for all those programme areas where the governments are policy-makers, project financiers, and/or decision-makers. Fourth, governments should clarify the objectives of their PPPs at all levels, in terms of baseline information for SEA. Finally, governments should adopt the 'environmental imperative', i.e. primacy for environmental goals, and give statutory force to this in the powers and duties of their ministers and agencies of state.

SEA is rapidly finding its way onto more and more political agendas, and the concept can be expected to remain on these agendas for many years to come. This is illustrated particularly well in the UK's SACTRA report (SACTRA, 1992), which argues that environmental concerns should play a greater part in the assessment of new road building programmes, and that environmental impacts should be assessed strategically. The British government has accepted that general principle, but now needs to act accordingly.

Worldwide, countries need to acknowledge both the strengths and weaknesses of SEA. SEA is not a universal panacea for global environmental problems, nor will it be easy to implement its theoretical potential within current institutional frameworks. However, the use of SEA is justified in terms of its consideration of alternatives, and cumulative and secondary effects of PPPs. SEA would allow explicit trade-offs to be made between objectives, and would achieve a more consistent integration of environmental concerns into decision-making. Each country has an important individual role to play in ensuring that SEA is carried out and that its conclusions are subsequently implemented, as well as its political and economic framework will allow. This must occur if the theory is to become reality.

Appendix A: Extracts from EC Directive 85/337

(shortened slightly from CEC, 1985)

A.1 Projects requiring EIA

'... projects of the classes listed in Annex I shall be made subject to an assessment...' (Article 4.1).

Annex I.

1. Crude oil refineries, facilities for the gasification and liquefaction of coal or bituminous shale.
2. Thermal power stations and other combustion installations with a heat output of 300 megawatts or more, and nuclear power stations and other nuclear reactors.
3. Installations for the permanent storage or disposal of radioactive waste.
4. Integrated works for the initial melting of cast-iron and steel.
5. Installations for the extraction, processing, and transformation of asbestos.
6. Integrated chemical installations.
7. Construction of motorways, express roads, lines for long-distance railway traffic and airports.
8. Ports and inland waterways.
9. Waste disposal installations for the incineration, chemical treatment or landfill of toxic and dangerous waste.

'Projects of the classes listed in Annex II shall be made subject to an assessment... where Member States consider that their characteristics so require. To this end Member States may *inter alia* specify certain types of projects as being subject to an assessment or may establish the criteria and/or thresholds necessary to determine which of the projects of the classes listed in Annex II are to be subject to an assessment...' (Article 4.2).

Annex II

1. *Agriculture*
   (a) Projects for restructuring rural land holdings.
   (b) Projects for the use of uncultivated land or semi-natural areas for intensive agricultural purposes.
   (c) Water management projects for agriculture.
   (d) Initial afforestation and land reclamation.

(e) Poultry-rearing installations.
(f) Pig-rearing installations.
(g) Salmon breeding.
(h) Reclamation of land from the sea.

2. *Extractive industry*
   (a) Extraction of peat.
   (b) Deep drillings.
   (c) Extraction of minerals other than metalliferous and energy-pro-ducing minerals.
   (d) Extraction of coal and lignite by underground mining.
   (e) Extraction of coal and lignite by open-cast mining.
   (f) Extraction of petroleum.
   (g) Extraction of natural gas.
   (h) Extraction of ores.
   (i) Extraction of bituminous shale.
   (j) Extraction of minerals other than metalliferous and energy-pro-ducing minerals by open-cast mining.
   (k) Surface industrial installations for the extraction of coal, petro-leum, natural gas, ores and bituminous shale.
   (l) Coke ovens.
   (m) Installations for the manufacture of cement.

3. *Energy industry*
   (a) Industrial installations for the production of electricity, steam and hot water (not in Annex I).
   (b) Industrial installations for carrying gas, steam and hot water; transmission of electrical energy by overhead cables.
   (c) Surface storage of natural gas.
   (d) Underground storage of combustible gases.
   (e) Surface storage of fossil fuels.
   (f) Industrial briquetting of coal and lignite.
   (g) Installations for the production or enrichment of nuclear fuels.
   (h) Installations for the reprocessing of nuclear fuels.
   (i) Installations for the collection and processing of radioactive waste (not in Annex I).
   (j) Installations for hydroelectric energy production.

4. *Processing of metals*
   (a) Iron and steelworks.
   (b) Installations for the production of non-ferrous metals.
   (c) Pressing, drawing and stamping of large castings.
   (d) Surface treatment and coating of metals.
   (e) Boilermaking, manufacture of sheet-metal containers.
   (f) Manufacture and assembly of motor vehicles.
   (g) Shipyards.

(*h*) Installations for the construction and repair of aircraft.
(*i*) Manufacture of railway equipment.
(*j*) Swaging by explosives.
(*k*) Installations for the roasting and sintering of metallic ores.

5. *Manufacture of glass*

6. *Chemical industry*
   (*a*) Treatment of intermediate products and production of chemicals (not in Annex I).
   (*b*) Production of pesticides and pharmaceutical products, paint, etc.
   (*c*) Storage facilities for petroleum, petrochemical and chemical products.

7. *Food industry*
   (*a*) Manufacture of vegetable and animal oils and fats.
   (*b*) Packing and canning of animal and vegetable products.
   (*c*) Manufacture of dairy products.
   (*d*) Brewing and malting.
   (*e*) Confectionery and syrup manufacture.
   (*f*) Installations for the slaughter of animals.
   (*g*) Industrial starch manufacturing installations.
   (*h*) Fish-meal and fish-oil factories.
   (*i*) Sugar factories.

8. *Textile, leather, wood and paper industries*
   (*a*) Wool scouring, degreasing and bleaching factories.
   (*b*) Manufacture of fibre board, particle board and plywood.
   (*c*) Manufacture of pulp, paper and board.
   (*d*) Fibre-dyeing factories.
   (*e*) Cellulose-processing and production installations.
   (*f*) Tannery and leather-dressing factories.

9. *Rubber industry*

10. *Infrastructure projects*
    (*a*) Industrial-estate development projects.
    (*b*) Urban development projects.
    (*c*) Ski-lifts and cable-cars.
    (*d*) Construction of roads, harbours, and airfields (not in Annex I).
    (*e*) Canalization and flood-relief works.
    (*f*) Dams.
    (*g*) Tramways, railways, suspended lines.
    (*h*) Oil and gas pipeline installations.
    (*i*) Installation of long-distance aqueducts.
    (*j*) Yacht marinas.

11. *Other projects*
  (*a*) Holiday villages, hotel complexes.
  (*b*) Permanent racing and test tracks for cars and motorcycles.
  (*c*) Installations for the disposal of industrial and domestic waste (not in Annex I).
  (*d*) Waste water treatment plants.
  (*e*) Sludge-depositions sites.
  (*f*) Storage of scrap iron.
  (*g*) Test benches for engines, turbines or reactors.
  (*h*) Manufacture of artificial mineral fibres.
  (*i*) Manufacture, etc. of gunpowder and explosives.
  (*j*) Knackers' yards.

12. Modifications to development projects included in Annex I and projects in Annex I undertaken exclusively or mainly for the development and testing of new methods or products and not used for more than one year.

A.2 Content of EIA

'In the case of projects which... must be subjected to an [EIA]... Member States shall adopt the necessary measures to ensure that the developer supplies in an appropriate form the information specified in Annex III inasmuch as:
(a) The Member States consider that the information is relevant...;
(b) the Member States consider that a developer may reasonably be required to compile this information...' (Article 5.1).

Annex III

1. Description of the project, including in particular:

  • a description of the physical characteristics of the whole project and the land-use requirements during the construction and operational phases,

  • a description of the main characteristics of the production processes,

  • an estimate, by type and quantity, of expected residues and emissions resulting from the operation of the proposed project.

2. Where appropriate, an outline of the main alternatives studied by the developer and an indication of the main reasons for his choice, taking into account the environmental effects.

3. A description of the aspects of the environment likely to be significantly affected by the proposed project, including, in particular, population, fauna, flora, soil, water, air, climatic factors, material assets, including the architectural and archaeological heritage, landscape and the inter-relationship between the above factors.

4. A description[1] of the likely significant effects of the proposed project on the environment resulting from:

    • the existence of the project,

    • the use of natural resources,

    • the emission of pollutants, the creation of nuisances and the elimination of waste;

    and a description by the developer of the forecasting methods used to assess the effects on the environment.

5. A description of the measures envisaged to prevent, reduce and where possible offset any significant adverse effects on the environment.

6. A non-technical summary of the information provided under the above headings.

7. An indication of any difficulties encountered by the developer in compiling the required information.

---

1. This description should cover the direct effects and any indirect, secondary, cumulative, short, medium and long-term, permanent and temporary, positive and negative effects of the project.

Appendix B: Critique of the proposed EC Directive on SEA, Policy Appraisal and the Environment, and Planning Policy Guidance Note 12

B.1 Proposed EC directive on SEA (CEC, 1991a)

Credits

A main benefit of the proposed directive is its legislative force. Once it is approved, Member States will be required to carry out its procedures. In this sense it differs from *Policy Appraisal and the Environment*, which is only a form of administrative guidance with no possibilities of enforcement. If the experience of EIA for projects holds true for PPPs, the proposed directive would trigger a large rise in the number and quality of SEAs carried out in the Member States.

The proposed directive would require the environment to be formally considered when the objectives and contents of PPPs are formulated; this is a powerful step towards the implementation of a framework for considering environmental impacts in decision making. In this sense, the proposed directive would affect the very heart of decision making.

The distinction that the proposed directive draws between the lead authority, competent authority and designated environmental authority is noteworthy. It provides good opportunity for a stringent review of the adequacy of SEAs and their recommendations. The requirement that the competent authority must publish reasons for its decisions is also likely to lead to better, more publicly accountable decisions.

The proposed directive would require the formal consideration of issues that are at present not considered or considered only marginally, particularly alternatives to PPPs and monitoring arrangements.

Criticisms

The proposed directive does not comprehensively cover PPPs. PPPs that are not likely to give rise to significant environmental effects or whose effects are taken into account at another stage of the planning process are exempted. Similarly, PPPs that are approved by a Cabinet decision and incorporate an EIA are exempted. Furthermore the list of PPPs usually requiring SEA does not include PPPs for such sectors as science and technology, industry and recreation. Finally, it makes preparation of an SEA discretionary for PPPs that are not implemented as projects, such as education, research and development, and fiscal policies.

The proposed directive is particularly weak in its consideration of environmental components, and relies overmuch on the list set out in Directive 85/337. It does not address any impacts related to sustainability, e.g. unique features, significant habitats, endangered species. Nor does it address impacts that may relate to other policies, or the broader policy-making context, e.g. risk and safety, services, waste disposal. Furthermore, it does not even consider 'interaction between the above impacts', which is included in Directive 85/337 (see Appendix A.2), and which in the case of project EIAs has been the justification for the consideration of such issues as ecology, agriculture and hydrology. It also does not list noise, which is considered in almost every project EIS, and is a major impact of PPPs relating to, for example, transport, industry and land use planning.

The proposed directive makes virtually no allowance for public consultation and participation, and certainly gives no guidance on how to encourage such participation, despite the fact that consultation with the public is one of its central objectives.

Finally, the proposed directive makes no mention of such basic principles as irreversibility, uncertainty, present versus future perceptions of value, or the precautionary principle. Sustainable development is addressed in the introduction to the proposed directive: 'Sustainable development depends on sound management of natural resources and on the preservation of the equilibrium of the different ecosystems.' But it is not listed as an objective of SEA.

B.2 Policy Appraisal and the Environment (DoE, 1991a)

Credits

The guide recognizes that the environmental effects of policy have sometimes been overlooked in government policy making, including both environmental policies as such, and those (such as defence, communications and taxation) that have environmental effects. The possibility of cumulative, secondary and indirect effects is also made explicit.

The guide emphasizes the value of making choices, such as the do-nothing option and trade-offs between objectives, more explicit. It offers scope for a clearer record of how decisions are made, and is realistic about the difficulties of policies 'growing out of' earlier decisions. It also brings out the importance of clarifying assumptions and the role of political judgement. It lays considerable stress on the acceptance of uncertainty (including scientific uncertainty and disagreement), and the need to adopt the precautionary principle.

Notwithstanding the critical comments below regarding valuation of the environment, the guide defines total economic value to include existence value, and accepts that certain elements may be more highly valued in the future, with rising expectations and diminishing environmental resources.

Criticisms

The guide makes little mention of sustainable development, which, as was discussed in chapter 7, should be the foundation for SEA.

Despite the guide's recognition that monetary valuation is not a valuation of environmental resources as such, but a measure of public preference, it relies over-much on the use of cost-benefit analysis through monetary evaluation or other forms of quantification. More than half of the total text concerns cost-benefit analysis, and the impression received by other government departments is that the guide is primarily a compendium of techniques for valuing environmental resources (Dowie, 1992). The emphasis placed on the different techniques for measuring preferences ignores the problem that the public will only reflect the society that has placed no, or too little, value on environmental goods.

The guide recognizes that the Treasury discount rate of 6 per cent should sometimes be reconsidered, but gives no clear guidance on how to ensure that the future worth of environmental resources is properly valued. Its recommendation to adjust assumptions about future values on a case-by-case basis gives insufficient weight to the nature of environmental issues. The guide is also too superficial in its concept of equivalent resources; for instance, no mention is made of the costs of adjustment over time.

It ostensibly sets out to integrate environmental costs and benefits better into government policy appraisal, but pays little attention to the initial steps (summarize the issue, list objectives, identify constraints and specify options). This effectively sidesteps perhaps the most important issues, namely the objectives of the policy, and the alternative policy options. It makes no attempt to suggest a weighting framework for policy making.

The possibility of consultation with the public or with interested groups is feebly addressed. There is reluctance to give weight to scientific or public opinions if there are pressures of time and confidentiality, and the suggestion that 'public concerns may be gauged initially by the correspondence received' is absurd.

The report is intended only as a guide, and places no clear obligation on its audience to implement its proposals. There is no evidence of external scrutiny of the use and implementation of the guide, and certainly no commitment to public availability of the results of agencies' appraisals under this system.

Finally, the guide accepts too readily the existing statutory procedures for project EIA. Recent reports (see chapter 1) have shown the inadequacies of many environmental statements, and many of their predictions are neither usable nor correct, and give an over-rosy view of a development's impacts.

B.3 Planning Policy Guidance Note 12 (DoE, 1992a)

Credits

PPG12 recognizes that policies in development plans *do* have a specific formulation process. Doubts expressed by central government about the continuous and iterative nature of policy formulation do not hold quite so firmly for development plans, which are subject to statutory procedures in terms of their preparation, content and form. In this sense, they are a suitable test-bed for the application of SEA.

Criticisms

One difficulty in implementing the PPG is the weight to be given to environmental considerations. If all policies in draft development plans are to be examined for their economic, social and environmental effects, the PPG gives no guidance as to how these are to be weighted. On the other hand, the definition of environmental appraisal that it gives *includes* analysis for financial, social and environmental effects.

The District Planning Officers' Society, in commenting on Susan Owens' report on Energy Conscious Planning (CPRE, 1991), found the concept of environmental appraisal of a development plan confusing:

> We oppose the proposal that, inter alia, development plans should be subject to environmental impact assessment. It is the essence of a development plan that it should consider all relevant factors, whether economic, social or environmental in shaping the policies and proposals. Thus the plan should derive from, among other things, environmental aims and assessments. To seek to apply environmental assessment to the resultant plan is to turn the process backwards, and serves no useful purpose. Apart from this objection in principle, the proposal is impractical since many of the proposals in a plan could only be assessed in relation to particular developers' proposals which would be unknown when the plan was prepared (DPOS, 1991).

Despite its reference to *Policy Appraisal and the Environment*, the PPG does not resolve this potential difficulty in appraising the policies that comprise a development plan when the plan itself, and its policies, may well be devised to achieve an objective of environmental protection or improvement.

A further problem is the requirement to include an account of this appraisal in the explanatory memorandum or reasoned justification for the development plan. If the appraisal is undertaken comprehensively and systematically as suggested, this account could be lengthy, and hence in conflict with the government's exhortation on the need for simplicity and brevity in plans.

There may also be a problem with the interpretation of the PPG as to whether its provisions for environmental appraisal apply to local plans as well as strategic plans. There is no provision in the PPG for it to apply to the policies in regional guidance, which constitutes a major (and no doubt deliberate) omission.

Questions also arise as to whether the policies that comprise the draft development plan can be appraised in isolation, policy-by-policy, as the PPG seems to imply. The shortcomings in information available for that appraisal, and the uncertainties surrounding the techniques of cost-benefit analysis or social cost-benefit analysis, for all the space devoted to them in *Policy Appraisal and the Environment*, remain.

Appendix C: Possible methodologies for strategic environmental assessment

C.1 Introduction and issues

As discussed in Chapter 2, the methodologies for undertaking SEA are neither well developed nor commonly agreed upon. It has not been the primary purpose of this book to present a treatment of methodologies, though it is a subject in need of urgent attention. There is a great paucity of guidance in existence: the best of what there is, is reviewed below, and some thoughts are offered on further application of SEA principles to practical situations.

Two issues in SEA methodology underlie many of the more specific techniques discussed in this appendix. First is the issue of whether SEA should take different forms for policies, plans, programmes and projects. Wood and Djeddour (1991) suggest that

> the vast majority of tasks involved in SEA are identical to those in project-level EIA. [And] it follows that many of the methods employed are directly transferable, though many will differ in degree of detail and level of specificity.

On the other hand, Street (1992) argues that policies, plans, programmes and projects have quite distinct characteristics, and that any system requiring the assessment of their environmental impacts should take these differences into account: EIA at more strategic levels by necessity is more broad-brush than at the project level, implying also that the issues considered at the different levels differ. Similarly, the proposed EC directive on SEA notes that:

> Which environmental impacts should be assessed at any given stage... and in which degree of detail, is a matter to be settled... For example, in the transport sector CO_2 impacts may be more meaningfully assessed when approving a national transport policy, plan or programme than when authorizing individual road schemes. On the other hand, the more localized impacts of CO_2 emissions may be more appropriately assessed at the project authorization stage (CEC, 1991a).

The second issue is whether SEA should take different forms depending on whether it concerns a regional, sectoral, or indirect PPP.

These issues have already become apparent when considering the main steps in SEA proposed by two of the most specific relevant guidelines: the manual prepared by the US Department of Housing and Urban Development (USHUD, 1981), and *Policy Appraisal and the Environment* (DoE, 1991a).

The USHUD manual was prepared specifically for 'areawide' (i.e. regional) SEA of plans and programmes, and proposes the following steps:

- determine need and feasibility of preparing an SEA;
- establish boundaries, analysis units and environmental database;
- identify alternatives;
- scoping;
- environmental analysis;
- impact synthesis and evaluation;
- recommendations.

Policy Appraisal and the Environment was prepared to assist in analysing the environmental impacts of policies of all types, and proposes the following steps:

- summarise the policy issue;
- list the objectives;
- identify the constraints;
- specify the options;
- identify the costs and benefits;
- weigh up the costs and benefits;
- test the sensitivity of the options;
- suggest the preferred option;
- set up any monitoring necessary;
- evaluate the policy at a later stage.

These are compared in Figure C.1. Policy analysis requires a discussion of policy issues, policy objectives, and policy constraints that is not necessary (or less feasible) at the plan or programme stage. This appendix is organized to incorporate a range of strategic levels and topics for SEA:

1. determining the need for an SEA;
2. establishing a work programme;
3. determining the objective(s) of the PPP;
4. defining the scope of the SEA;
5. environmental analysis;
6. establishing an environmental database;
7. impact evaluation and synthesis;
8. proposing recommendations and preparing an SEA report;
9. monitoring and feedback.

Figure C.1 Steps in SEA methodology
(DoE, 1991a; USHUD, 1981)

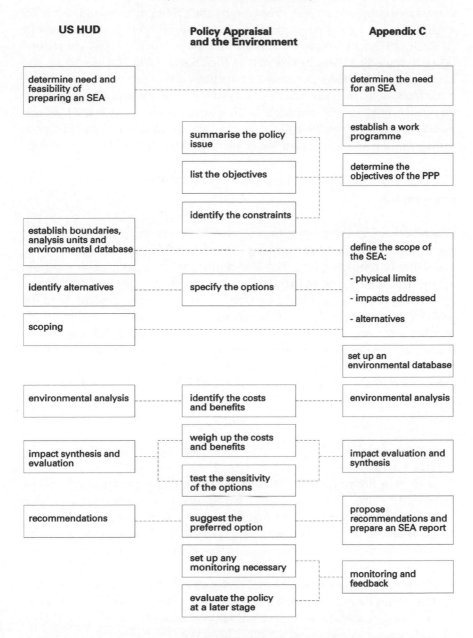

| US HUD | Policy Appraisal and the Environment | Appendix C |

Although a step-by-step methodology is proposed, these steps do not necessarily occur in strict sequential order. Furthermore the steps in the procedure should be regarded as components of an iterative process, requiring comment by the public and feedback into the process.

The Appendix is drawn substantially from the USHUD manual

(USHUD, 1981) and *Policy Appraisal and the Environment* (DoE, 1991a). It also draws on existing SEAs and other sources. Throughout, it refers by way of an example to an SEA prepared by the US Department of Energy on a programme of environmental restoration and waste management (USDOE, 1992c). In this context, environmental restoration refers to actions taken to remedy the environment and facilities at USDOE sites across the US to ensure that risks from past operations are either eliminated or reduced to safe levels (this includes assessing conditions and cleaning facilities contaminated with radioactive, hazardous and mixed waste). Waste management involves the collection, storage, destruction or stabilization, transportation and disposal of waste produced by the USDOE's activities.

C.2 Determining the need for strategic environmental assessment

The first stage in the preparation of an SEA is for the lead authority (or agency) to decide whether there is a need for an SEA and to determine the feasibility of preparing one. The lead agency is the agency proposing the action. This is comparable to the developer or the agency granting the permit in project EIA (Wood and Djeddour, 1991). In some cases, the need for SEA will be determined by legislation, such as that discussed in Chapter 3. In other cases, agencies will prepare SEAs to improve their efficiency, environmental sensitivity, or 'green' credentials. The decision as to whether or not to prepare an SEA will often be a political one. However, certain factors can be identified that would suggest that an SEA is needed. For instance, to determine the need for areawide assessment, the USHUD have developed four broad questions:

1. Is there a high level of government or other agency activity within the study area?
2. Is there a high rate of change in the area, e.g. population growth or housing starts, that will trigger demand for future services? A high growth rate may trigger concerns that can be addressed by an SEA.
3. How significant is public sector action to the area? For example are there government policies or programmes that could result in a concentration of activity in the area?
4. Are there unique environmental features or sensitive sites in the area? This could include concerns such as a high rate of loss of key resources or persistent violations of environmental standards.

C.3 Establishing a work programme

After deciding that an SEA is required, the lead agency should establish a work programme for the SEA. This would include a discussion of the goals that are to be achieved by undertaking the SEA, and a list of tasks that are essential to the SEA. It would also discuss internal administrative matters that would need to be addressed, including the schedule, budget and staff for the operation. More specifically, it could address:

- goals, issues and problems;

- tasks to be addressed:

    public participation programme;
    consultations with relevant experts and providers of data;
    establishment and/or updating of existing database;
    summarizing of relevant policy, plans, objectives and scenarios;
    carrying out of scoping exercises;
    performance of detailed impact assessment;
    summarizing of comments and responses;
    preparation of implementation plan;
    documentation of results in final SEA report;
    monitoring and feedback.

- budget, timetable and products;

- staffing plan;

- cooperating agencies (USHUD, 1981).

The budget for an SEA is often limited; the present climate of tight government constraints on spending, and other conflicting statutory obligations will mean that the lead agency will need to justify the time and money required for SEA. In developing countries, those problems may be exacerbated by issues such as famine and debt burdens. Funds will have to be carefully allocated to maximize the SEA's effectiveness. The costs of carrying out SEA could be minimized by judicious scoping, and by limiting the scale of data collection to the minimum necessary. However, this may allow SEA to be marginalized to the point that it is not able radically to question existing policies owing to a lack of information and funding (Pickles, 1992).

C.4 Determining the objective(s) of the PPP

SEA should be based on a clear understanding of the objectives of the policy, plan or programme in question. Many PPPs will incorporate environmental considerations (see for example Box 5.1 for objectives of the UK's energy policy) but as a part of a broader, and perhaps internally conflicting, set of objectives. Other PPPs may be inherently environmental in nature (see for example Appendix B concerning the discussion surrounding the objectives of development).

In particular the ultimate objectives (those which the [PPP] seeks to achieve) should be distinguished from the intermediate objectives (the means by which the ultimate objectives are to be achieved). This will allow the trade-off between different classes of objectives to be made explicit. Each objective should be revisited during the course of the appraisal in the light of the analysis of the options. A slight reshaping of the objectives may have a significant effect on the impacts and on the trade-offs (DoE, 1991a).

It is this stage that sets the framework within which subsequent decisions will be made: ideally, sustainability should be incorporated as an ultimate objective of the PPP (see chapter 7).

C.5 Defining the scope of the strategic environmental assessment

The scoping process is a crucial preliminary review of all environmental components of impact categories and how that PPP might affect them, as well as the amount of attention to be given to the analysis of potential impacts. The scope of each SEA will differ according to its level (policy, plan or programme), its type (sectoral, regional, indirect), where it is being carried out and by whom. Defining the scope involves the identification of the physical/regional limits of the assessment, of the impacts that it will address, and of the possible alternatives it will cover. It must also consider constraints such as legislative requirements, the need for mitigation or compensation, and the views of the public and relevant organizations.

There are no fixed rules for *identifying the physical or regional limits of an SEA*. For programme or plan level SEA, they will generally be influenced by two sets of factors. The first is existing features of the geography of the area, such as natural resource features (e.g. drainage basins, mountain ranges) or boundaries established by human-made features (e.g. motorways, railways, canals). The second is existing administrative boundaries, such as local planning authority boundaries (USHUD, 1981). Ordnance Survey maps and overlay mapping techniques can be useful at this stage. There will be cases where boundaries will be established solely for the purpose of undertaking the SEA.

For policy SEA the boundaries will be jurisdictional, and will involve the lead agency deciding how much and what level of influence the related government departments should be given, after inter-departmental consultation.

Once an area boundary has been defined, and depending on the size of the study area, it may be necessary to break the area into smaller sized 'analysis' units for ease of data collection. The USHUD (1981) proposes the following types of analysis units:

- arbitrary grids designed to be compatible with computerized databases;

- traffic analysis zones based on census and local jurisdictional boundaries;

- census geographical boundaries;

- jurisdictional boundaries (e.g. city, county);

- natural system boundaries (e.g. drainage basins, aquifer recharge zones).

For instance an areawide SEA for a 29,200 ha growth corridor in Delaware (US) adjacent to a highway defined six analysis units based on traffic zone boundaries (USHUD, 1981). A plan SEA for 373,600 ha in California defined 11 'analysis units' that were identified solely for data management and planning purposes and did not correspond to any specific type of jurisdiction (Baseline Environmental Consulting, 1991).

The process of *identifying relevant impacts to be addressed in the SEA* could include the use of checklists, a review of existing data and a comparison with alternative options to highlight any significant impacts, and the circulation of a preliminary list of impacts to staff and/or the public for an interdisciplinary review of the issues.

There are established lists available of environmental components or impact categories that are likely to feature in an SEA (e.g. CEC, 1991a; HUD, 1981; State of California, 1986); some of these are shown in Chapter 3. Other impact identification lists and matrices can be adapted from methodologies for project EIA (e.g. CEC, 1985; Leopold, 1971). These should be seen as a guide to the likely impacts that the lead agency will need to consider. The development of a set of quantitative descriptors for each alternative may prove useful, since the descriptors will ultimately serve as the basic inputs to impact assessment calculations.

Identifying the alternatives covered is one of the most crucial steps of the SEA. A full treatment of the rationale for selecting, ranking and rejecting any alternatives is essential for any thorough SEA. Transparency in these decisions is crucial to the confidence that will be expected of those using or having to accept the SEA. Substantial judgement will be needed in identifying alternatives, owing to the political sensitivity of many alternatives and because of the influence of assumptions made on future development patterns at the outset.

Alternatives should represent a range of more or less likely development outcomes for the study area, based on the best information at hand, including the 'do nothing' option. Methodologies that can be used for generating alternatives include intuitive techniques, forecasting based on discussions by subject specialists, cost-benefit analysis, goals achievement matrix analysis, and lists of standards (Wood, 1988). An example of the alternatives considered in a programme-level SEA is presented in Box C.1.

The scoping process should be carried out in a climate of *openness and public accountability*. Public participation and the co-operation of other relevant agencies should be encouraged. Box C.2 gives an example of public participation in the scoping process. Once this has been carried out, the results of the process should be recorded, and the study design amended accordingly.

Box C.1 Identifying alternatives in SEA
(USDOE, 1992c)

The SEA for the environmental restoration and waste management programme prepared by the US Department of Energy (1992c) provides an example of how alternatives can be considered in an SEA. The SEA examines the potential environmental consequences of various alternative courses of action for achieving an integrated environmental restoration and waste management programme. Alternatives are proposed for environmental restoration activities, waste management activities and spent nuclear fuel management.

For *environmental restoration*, alternatives considered are:
1. 'no new action' alternative (the current course of action);
2. reliance on engineering and institutional controls;
3. reliance on removal and treatment;
4. a combination of controls and treatment.

For *waste management activities*, alternatives are considered for six categories of waste: high-level waste; transuranic waste; low-level waste; low-level mixed waste; greater-than-class-C low level waste and hazardous waste. For each of the six categories the USDOE will consider three alternatives:
1. 'no new action' alternative (the current programme);
2. minimum consolidation;
3. maximum consolidation.

(Consolidation refers to storing the waste and spent nuclear fuel at a reduced number of sites, which minimises the amount of land used, but increases transportation activity.) The same three alternatives apply to *spent nuclear fuel management*.

For each alternative the following are evaluated: transportation risk (collision, shipment and spillage); risk from construction, operation and effluent release at the treatment facility; impacts on land, water, energy and use of construction materials; potential for recycling; impacts on air quality, noise, biological resources, socio-economic factors, archaeological interests, surface- and groundwater; near-term risk (including industrial, radiological and hazardous material), and residual risk (including the cumulative risk to the public from exposure to radioactive and hazardous material).

The principal discerning factor between the alternatives is the amount of transportation and the use of land for treatment, storage and disposal facilities. The analysis for this SEA is primarily qualitative and the results of the analysis will be descriptive using standard modelling.

Box C.2 Public participation in SEA scoping
(USDOE, 1992c)

The US Department of Energy's 1992 SEA for an environmental restoration and waste management programme provides an example of public participation in scoping. The scoping process began by the Department of Energy publishing a *Notice of Intent* (NOI) which:

- defined the proposed action;

- defined alternative actions;

- established issues to be considered within the SEA;

- established issues outwith the SEA's remit.

The NOI invited the public and government agencies to provide written comment on the scope of the SEA and/or to participate in scoping meetings. Approximately one month later a *national workshop* was held with representatives from environmental and public interest groups, to discuss the proposed scope of the SEA and ways to improve public participation. This resulted in a revision to the original scoping meeting plan, and agreements to distribute written material prior to public meetings and allocate time for informal interaction between those planning to attend and the USDOE.

The *scoping meetings* were announced by official US government notices and in the local media. In all, for this one SEA, 23 scoping meetings were held in locations across the US between December 1990 and February 1991. Transcripts of the proceedings were made available. Seven thousand comments were received from 1200 members of the public; these included both verbal and written comments. The majority were from individuals, with 280 organizations submitting responses.

In order to facilitate evaluation of the comments, the USDOE developed a *comments tracking system*. Comments were organized according to keywords: when a single comment raised more than one issue, multiple keywords were assigned. As a result the USDOE identified 15,000 keyword comments in total, which were categorized into 24 issues. For example clean-up levels and land use received 402 keyword comments, environmental quality and environmental impact received 1840 comments, occupational and public health received 1681 comments and transportation issues received 349 comments. For each of the 24 issues raised, the USDOE published examples of the range of comments made by the public and its response to the issues raised.

This information was in turn made available for public review and comment. Regional interactive workshops have also been planned to incorporate additional public comments on the process.

C.6 Environmental analysis

After the scope of the SEA has been agreed, baseline data are collected, impacts are predicted and their significance is evaluated, and mitigation measures are proposed. To assist in these steps, an environmental database will need to be set up: this is discussed in section C.7.

Knowledge of the *baseline situation* is a necessary reference point against which to predict and then monitor any environmental change that may occur. It is essential that provisions for assembling baseline data, and data collection should be initiated at an early stage in the process (Wathern, 1988). Often the policy, plan or programme will also not be new, but rather a modification of an existing one: it will thus be possible to monitor the effects that the existing policy is having; this will provide useful baseline information for the SEA (Pickles, 1992).

A plethora of agencies and organizations can be contacted regarding environmental data (see, for example Adatia and Gibson (1992) for UK organizations concerned with the environment, and the Department of Trade and Industry (1992) for UK government departments concerned with environmental issues). There will also generally be a large amount of existing environmental data relating to the study area. This may include, for instance, information from authorities responsible for water quality or habitat protection, from environmental audits, or from existing land use plans. However, this information will often not be comprehensive or in the form that is wanted, and further manipulation may be necessary.

The first step should be to decide what data will be required and establish what is already in existence. Existing environmental data can be collated and gaps in information can be identified using existing maps and aerial photographs, data collation and retrieval systems, and consultation with specialist agencies. Monitoring systems and special surveys (using, for example, aerial photography or field sampling) can be used to obtain additional environmental data to meet remaining deficiencies (Wood, 1988).

Impact prediction techniques for SEA will not need to be as specific as for project EIA. Techniques that can provide information for wide areas of the country include aerial photography, cartographic techniques, computer models and national and regional forecasts relating to issues such as population, energy use, pollution levels and traffic (Pickles, 1992). Other techniques for impact prediction include mapping and overlay methods, resource and waste coefficient analyses, accident and uncertainty analysis, and consultation with other agencies and the public (Wood, 1988). Cumulative, secondary and indirect impacts particularly need to be addressed.

Evaluation of the significance of the impact can be based on such criteria as compliance with relevant environmental standards, maintenance of carrying capacities, and sensitivity to local residents' views. The following methodologies may be useful in predicting the magnitude and significance of environmental impacts: checklists; scaling and weighting systems; overlay methods; consultation with environmental agencies; screening procedures; resource depletion; diffusion and damage analysis; and landscape assessment techniques (Wood, 1988; CEC, 1991a). Compliance with environmental quality standards may be tested using lists of standards and social surveys.

Mitigation measures should be proposed to eliminate or minimize all negative environmental impacts identified in previous steps of the SEA. Such measures could include:

- changing (part of) the PPP's scale, type, or general location (e.g. higher density urban development, recycling or recovery of resulting waste);

- improved public outreach (e.g. advisory groups, public information programmes);

- changing the objectives of the PPP (e.g. revising cost-benefit frameworks to give greater weight to non-quantifiable impacts);

- compensation, be it financial or otherwise (e.g. establishment of nature reserves, community centres, improved transport infrastructure, or other 'shadow projects' (see Pearce et al., 1989));

- as a last resort, resettling or reconstructing of the affected population or habitat (e.g. reconstruction of wetlands).

Many of these mitigation methods will be an extension of mitigation at the project level.

Box C.3 illustrates the methodology for environmental analysis proposed in the USHUD guidebook on SEA, focusing on the example of 'significant habitats and species' (the full list of impacts addressed by the guidebook is given at Section 3.1). The guidebook provides specific steps to be followed for each of the environmental components identified as being significant to the SEA, under the following headings:

- issues which need to be addressed;

- assessment questions;

- baseline data;

- impact assessment techniques;

- evaluation;

- mitigation measures;

- references.

Box C.3 **Example of USHUD environmental analysis techniques concerning significant habitats and species**
(adapted and shortened from USHUD, 1981)

Issues that need to be addressed

The issues that need to be addressed in an SEA regarding significant habitats and species include a description of the dependence of flora and fauna on environmental conditions; their ability to adapt to human induced change; the interrelationship between development and the environment; measures that can minimize adverse environmental impact; the value of species to humans; and the role they play within the ecosystem. Impacts on the following need to be addressed:

- sensitive or protected species or habitats;

- interrelationships between post-PPP human population and local plant and animal life;

- threats to habitats and species with high economic, recreational or aesthetic and cultural value;

- areas of high natural resource or economic value.

Assessment questions

These are based on those issues which have been highlighted above:

- What is the existing ecological make up of the study area?

- What species or habitats exist in the area and are threatened, endangered or locally unique or have an economic, recreational or aesthetic/cultural value?

- What impact will development have on existing ecosystems?

- What ecosystems will survive or emerge in the developed area?

Baseline data

This lists relevant sources of baseline data, including the Fish and Wildlife Service, Army Corps of Engineers, and state natural resource agencies.

Impact assessment techniques

These involve establishing existing conditions, identifying critical ecological areas and defining the likely future conditions in the study area. The baseline environmental conditions of the area need to be defined, and the results mapped. A wildlife biologist should prepare an indigenous species list, indicating population sizes, spatial distribution, biomass and habitat productivity. Historical data and remote sensing information should be examined to identify areas that are required for feeding, nesting and other behavioural requirements of the various species, including species lower in the food chain.

The impacts of the PPP should then be described and where possible quantified. The location of areas critical to the survival of sensitive species should be described in relation to the area that will be developed. Areas should be set aside for species designated as important, or necessary to maintain the ecological integrity of the area. The expected ecological make up of the area after development should be estimated. The likely succession of the ecological community post-PPP should be compared with existing predictions.

Evaluation

Wildlife and conservation organizations should be contacted for information regarding evaluation of development impacts on sensitive habitats. The legal requirements relating to the environment and conservation should be examined and taken into account. Goals should be established against which development proposals can be evaluated at a later stage.

Mitigation measures

Habitats and the resources necessary for survival of sensitive species should be provided either by not developing on these habitats or by providing new habitats as part of the development. Specific mitigation measures include building higher density development that allows more land to remain in its natural state; purchase of sensitive habitats by a public agency or conservation organization; zoning to prevent development within a certain distance of a sensitive habitat or species and, if possible and desirable, relocation of species.

C.7 Establishing an environmental database

The success of SEA largely depends on the availability of environmental data, in a form that is accessible and of a nature and on a scale that is appropriate to the area being studied. A database will need to be established to deal with the large amounts of information generated and manipulated during impact analysis, synthesis, evaluation and monitoring.

Management of the database can range from simple paper files and overlay maps to more sophisticated computer storage systems with computerized mapping. The level of precision that can be demanded of the database will depend on the level of precision of the data input and the output required.

Geographical Information Systems (GIS) can be particularly useful in modelling and predicting changes to the environment. In Scotland, for instance, the sieving, mapping and filter capabilities of GIS have proven valuable in the production by regional councils of Integrated Forestry Strategies; these identify areas that are deemed to have forestry potential and suggest areas unsuitable for planting (Davidson, 1992). GIS files could be used as part of the SEA report, to allow alternative options to be compared: this requires that government or management authorities have the organizational structures to enable GIS to play an integral role in decision making (Davidson, 1992). Similarly, Stern (1990) proposes that a centralized institution could be established to identify the location, content and means of public access to existing information regarding health and the environment within a region using GIS.

The amount of data that might conceivably be relevant to any SEA is enormous. For instance, Pickles (1992) notes that there are between 2000 and 4000 species of invertebrates in the UK; mapping the occurrence of these species is already difficult, but a proper ecological survey would also consider, for instance, the time of year when these species are active. It will be necessary to avoid overcollection of data and to devise techniques that allow identification of the point at which valid conclusions can be drawn without the need for further data collection.

Data requirements can be kept to manageable levels by using scoping to identify the most important impacts and exclude the more minor ones.

C.8 Impact evaluation and synthesis

The evaluation of the impacts of various alternative options should take into account not only raw data on impacts, but also other considerations necessary to interpret and evaluate these data. These include regulatory standards, government guidance, the attitudes and preferences of residents, and the effectiveness of public planning and management in mitigating potential impacts through prevention, reduction and compensation.

Evaluation of alternatives could take the form of a matrix, with the various alternatives listed on the horizontal axis, and environmental components on the vertical axis: the scale and importance of the relevant alternative on each environmental component would be noted in the appropriate matrix cell.

C.9 Proposing recommendations and preparing an SEA report

Recommendations will be derived from the findings of the impact evaluation. These may include:

- the identification of a preferred alternative;

- mitigation measures;

- monitoring measures that may be necessary.

Techniques that could be used in the light of SEA findings to select a PPP for implementation, from among a choice of alternatives, include the application of evaluation criteria (see section C.8), public participation, and consultation with other agencies (Wood, 1988).

Often impacts will have to be evaluated despite a level of uncertainty concerning their likelihood or risk. *Policy Appraisal and the Environment* advocates the use of the so-called 'precautionary approach' in evaluating impacts:

> Where there is no prospect of resolving [uncertainty regarding impacts] policy should be constructed around it... Where there are significant chances of damage to the environment, [the government] is prepared to take a precautionary approach even where the scientific knowledge is not conclusive, though the economic costs of the action must not be greater than is commensurate with the nature and degree of risk involved (DoE, 1991a).

The guidebook also advocates the use of pilot projects and contingency plans to reduce the level of uncertainty and of risk posed by this uncertainty. As was discussed at chapter 7, carrying capacities and sustainability should provide fundamental criteria by which to evaluate impacts; distinctions should be made between short-term and long-term impacts, and reversible and irreversible impacts.

A formal *SEA report* should then be prepared and made available, documenting the findings of each stage of the process. It should include:

- description of the need for, and objectives for, the SEA;

- discussion of the objective(s) of the PPP;

- description of the existing policies and regulations affecting the SEA;

- explanation of the scoping process and its conclusions;

- discussion of the alternatives considered, and rationale for selecting preferred option(s);

- description of the existing environment and, if appropriate, the area likely to be affected;

- description of the significant impacts of the preferred PPP and of the alternatives considered;

- mitigation measures discussed and proposed;
- details of monitoring proposed;
- difficulties encountered in each stage of the process, including technical problems, information deficits, or lack of methodological knowledge;
- details of consultees;
- provisions for, and results of, public participation exercises;
- a non-technical summary of the report.

(Adapted from Wood and Djeddour, 1991.)

The SEA findings could be reported using overlays, mapping, photomontages, models, matrices and summary sheets as well as text.

C.10 Monitoring and feedback

Finally, monitoring will be needed to evaluate the effects of the policy, identify further studies and modifications needed during implementation, and feed back into future decision making.

> It is important to check the extent to which the assumptions and forecasts in the [SEA] have turned out to be valid in the event. This process can be used both to confirm the validity of the policy choices and to inform future decisions (DoE, 1991a).

Monitoring techniques could include the application of evaluation criteria and use of guidelines, consultation and public participation, and environmental monitoring systems (CEC, 1991a). In California, all EIAs must include a section that discusses, for each significant impact identified, recommended mitigation measures, monitoring requirements, the person or agency responsible for monitoring the mitigation measure, and the timing or frequency of monitoring (State of California, 1986; Baseline Environmental Consulting, 1991).

REFERENCES

Adatia, R. and Gibson, B. (1992) *Who's Who in the Environment*, The Environmental Council, London.

Anderson, F.R., Mandelker, D.R. and Tarlock, A.D. (1984) *Environmental Protection: Law and Policy*, Little, Brown and Company, Boston.

Andrews, J. and Auld, M. (1989) 'Taking the Initiative', *Birds Magazine*, RSPB, Autumn, pp. 38-40.

Association for the Conservation of Energy (1992) '"E" for Efficiency', *The Fifth Fuel*, 26, p.3.

Auld, M. (1991) 'Action for Heathlands', *Birds Magazine*, RSPB, Summer, pp. 39-40.

Auld, M., Pickess, B.P. and Burgess, N.D. (1990) 'Proceedings of Heathland Conference II – History and Management of Southern Lowland Heaths', Dorset, 4-6 June, RSPB.

Bachtold, H-G. (1991) *Computer-Aided Energy Planning as an Aspect of Urban Planning*, presented to the AESOP/ACSP Conference on Planning Transatlantic: Global Change and Local Problems, Oxford Polytechnic, Oxford.

Ball, S. and Bell, S. (1991) *Environmental Law*, Blackstone Press Ltd, London.

Bailey, R. (1991) 'Energy Policy in Confusion', *National Westminster Bank Quarterly Review*, February.

Barnes, M. (1990) *The Hinkley Point Public Inquiries: A Report to the Secretaries of State for Energy and the Environment*, HMSO, London.

Barrett, B.D.F. and Therivel, R. (1991) *Environmental Policy and Impact Assessment in Japan*, Routledge, London.

Barrett, S. and Fudge, C., eds., (1981) *Policy and Action*, Methuen, London.

Barton, H. (1990) 'Local Global Planning', *The Planner* 76(42), pp. 12-15.

Barton, H. (1991) *City Transport: Strategies for Sustainability*, presented to the BSRSA Conference, Oxford.

Baseline Environmental Consulting (1991) *Draft Environmental Impact Report on the San Joaquin County Comprehensive Planning Program ER 91-3*, prepared for San Joaquin County Community Development Department, California.

Bass, R. (1990) 'California's Experience with Environmental Impact Reports', *Project Appraisal*, pp. 220-4.

Bass, R. (1991) 'Policy, Plan and Programme EIA in California', *EIA Newsletter* 5, pp. 4-5.

Bass, R. and Herson, A.I. (1991) *California Environmental Law and Land Use Practice*, Chapters 20-3 'The California Environmental Quality Act', Matthew Bender & Co., Inc., Sacramento, CA.

Bausch, C. (1991) 'Achieving NEPA's Purpose in the 1990s', *The Environmental Professional* 13, pp. 95-9.

Bear, D. (1990) 'EIA in the USA after Twenty Years of NEPA', *EIA Newsletter* 4, EIA Centre, University of Manchester.

Bidwell, R. (1992) 'Sustainability: the Link between Conservation and Economic Benefits', *Environmental Impact Assessment Review* 12(1/2), pp. 37-48

Binnie & Partners (1991) *Water for the Future in Kent*, Binnie & Partners, Surrey.

Bisset, R. and Tomlinson, P. (1988) 'Monitoring and Auditing of Impacts', Chapter 7 in P. Wathern, ed., *Environmental Impact Assessment*, Unwin Hyman, London.

Braun, C. (1992) Department of the Environment, personal communication, 10 February.

Breakell, M. (1990) 'Starting from Scratch on Resource Management', *Planning* 855, p. 30.

Bristol Energy and Environment Plan (1992) *Sustainable Transport for Bristol*, BEEP, Bristol.

Budd, W.W. (1992) 'What Capacity the Land?' *Journal of Soil and Water Conservation* 47(1), pp. 28-31.

Burgon, J. (1992) National Trust, personal communication, 3 February.

Cabrera, P.R. (1984) *Environmental Impact Assessment in the Third World*, PhD thesis, University of Reading.

Cadbury, C.J. (1991) 'What Future for Lowland Heaths in Southern Britain?' *Conservation Review* 13, RSPB, pp. 61-7.

Cadbury, J. and Moore, N. (1989) 'Heathland Wildlife – Rare Essentials', *Birds Magazine*, RSPB, Autumn, pp. 16-20.

Churchill, R., Warren, L. and Gibson, J. (1991) *Law, Policy and the Environment*, Basil Blackwell, Oxford.

Clark, M. and Herington, J. eds. (1988) *The Role of Environmental Impact Assessment in the Planning Process*, Mansell, London.

Coalfields Communities Campaign (1992) *The Case Against Gas*, Barnsley.

Coles, T.F. and Tarling, J. (1991) 'Environmental Assessment: Experience to Date', Institute of Environmental Assessment.

Coles, T.F., Fuller, K.G. and Tarling, J. (1992) 'Environmental Assessment: Experience in the UK', paper presented at first membership conference, Institute of Environmental Assessment, Birmingham, 6 July.

Commission of the European Communities (1985) 'Directive on the Assessment of the Effects of Certain Private and Public Projects' (85/337/EEC), *Official Journal of the European Communities* 175, Brussels.

Commission of the European Communities (1987) *Fourth Action Programme on the Environment*, COM(86)485 Final, 9 Oct.

Commission of the European Communities (1991a) 'Draft Proposal for Directive on the Environmental Assessment of Policies, Plans and Programmes', XI/194/90-EN-REV.4, Brussels, 4 June.

Commission of the European Communities (1991b) 'A Review of the Implementation of Directive 85/337/EEC', Contract No. 6610(90)8685.

Commission of the European Communities (1991c) 'Report to UN Conference on Environment and Development', SEC(91)2448.

Commission of the European Communities (1992) *Towards Sustainability: Fifth Action Programme on the Environment*, CEC.

Commission on Energy and the Environment (1981) *Coal and the Environment*, HMSO, London.

Contant, C.K. and Wiggins, L.L. (1991) 'Defining and Analysing Cumulative Environmental Impacts', *Environmental Impact Assessment Review* 11(4), pp. 297-309.

Cope, D. (1991) 'Coal and Nuclear Research and Development', *UK CEED Bulletin* 35, pp. 8-9.

Cope, D., Hills, P. and James, P., eds. (1984) *Energy Policy and Land-Use Planning*, Pergamon Press, Oxford.

Couch, W.J. (1991) 'Recent EIA Developments in Canada', *EIA Newsletter* 6, pp. 17-18.

Council for the Protection of Rural England (1991) *The Environmental Assessment Directive – Five Years On*, CPRE, London.

Council of Europe (1977) Committee of Ministers Resolution 77(5) on the Conservation and Management of Heathlands, Strasbourg.

Cowart, R.H. (1986) 'Vermont's Act 250 After 15 Years', *Environmental Impact Assessment Review* 6, pp. 140-1.

Crown Estates Commission (1989) 'Marine Fish Farming in Scotland – Development Strategy and Guidelines', CEC.

Culley, G. (1992) English Nature, personal communication, 20 February.

Davidson, D.A (1992) 'GIS and Environmental Management', *European Environment*, 2(3), pp. 13-17.

Davies, S. (1989a) 'The Battle for Canford Heath', *Birds Magazine*, RSPB, Autumn, pp 30-5.

Davies, G.H. (1989b) 'Heathland – England's Own Disaster Area', *Birds Magazine*, RSPB, Autumn, pp 6-8.

de Jongh, P. (1991) 'Environmental Policy Plans and EIA: The Dutch Experience', *EIA Newsletter* 5, pp. 3-4.

Department of Energy (1990) *An Evaluation of Energy Related Greenhouse Gases Emissions and Measures to Ameliorate Them*, Energy Paper No. 58, HMSO, London.

Department of Energy (1991) *Digest of UK Energy Statistics 1991*, HMSO, London.

Department of Energy et al. (1992) *The Government's Expenditure Plans within the Energy Sector 1992-93 to 1994-95*, Cm 1905, HMSO, London.

Department of the Environment (1989) *Environmental Assessment: A Guide to the Procedures*, HMSO, London.

Department of the Environment (1991a) *Policy Appraisal and the Environment*, HMSO, London.

Department of the Environment (1991b) news release, 28 October.

Department of the Environment (1991c) *Monitoring Environmental Assessment and Planning*, HMSO, London.

Department of the Environment (1992a) *PPG12: Development Plans and Regional Planning Guidance*, HMSO, London.

Department of the Environment (1992b) *Joint Circular from the DoE, Welsh Office; Planning Controls Over Sites of Special Scientific Interest*, 2 January, DoE.

Department of the Environment (1992c) *Draft PPG on Coastal Planning*, DoE.

Department of the Environment (1992d) *Draft PPG on Renewable Energy*, DoE.

Department of the Environment (1992e) *Consultation Paper on Environmental Assessment and Planning: Extension of Application*, 30 June, London.

Department of the Environment (1992f) *Draft PPG on Nature Conservation*, DoE.

Department of Trade and Industry (1992) *Environmental Contacts; A guide for business – Who does what in government departments*, HMSO, London.

Department of Transport (1989) *Roads for Prosperity*, Cm 693, HMSO, London.

Department of Transport (1990) *Trunk Roads, England: Into the 1990s*, HMSO, London.

Department of Transport (1992a) *The Government's Response to the SACTRA Report on Assessing the Environmental Impact of Road Schemes*, HMSO, London.

Department of Transport (1992b) *The Government's Expenditure Plans for Transport 1992-93 to 1994-95*, Cm 1907, HMSO, London.

Devon County Council (1991) 'Devon County Structure Plan', Devon County Council.

Devon County Council (1992) 'Exe Estuary Management Plan', County Engineering and Planning Dept.

Dickert, T.G. and Tuttle, A.E. (1985) 'Cumulative Impact Assessment in Environmental Planning', *Environmental Impact Assessment Review* 5, pp. 37-64.

District Planning Officers' Society (1991) *Observations of the Society on Energy-Conscious Planning, Report of the CPRE*, DPOS.

Dixon, J.A., Carpenter, R.A., Fallon, L.A., Sherman, P.B. and Manipomoke, S. (1986) *Economic Analysis of the Environmental Impacts of Development Projects*, Earthscan, London.

Dorset Heathland Forum (1990) 'Dorset Heathland Strategy', Dorset County Council.

Dowie, J. (1992) Department of Energy, personal communication, 24 February.

Drewett, J. (1991) 'Action for Staffordshire Heathlands', Proceedings of the Conference, 14 March 1991.

Ebrahimi, A. (1992) *Energy Trends: A Historical Overview*, unpublished.

Ebrahimi, A. and Elliott, G. (1992) 'Energy Policy and Bird Species', *Ecos* 12(4), pp. 21-28.

EIA Newsletter, EIA Centre, University of Manchester, Manchester.

ENDS Report (1991) 'Opening Shots in the Debate on Strategic Environmental Assessment', 196, pp. 18-20.

English Nature (1992) *Observation on the government's draft PPG on Renewable Energy*, Peterborough.

Environment Business (1992) 'Environmental Protection Act 1990 Part I', supplement, January.

Enyedi, G., Gijswijt, A. and Rhode, B., eds. (1987) *Environmental Policies in East and West*, Taylor Graham, London.

European Bank for Reconstruction and Development (1992) *Environmental Procedures*, EBRD, London.

European Information Service (1991) Environment Section, 11 November 1991.

Farrell, L. (1983) *Focus on Nature. Conservation No 2. Heathland Management. A Report of the Heathland Habitat Network Meeting Held at Furzebrook Research Station, Dorset*, 12-13 November 1981, NCC.

Fells, I. and Lucas, N. (1992) 'UK Energy Policy Post-Privatization', *Energy Policy* 20(5), pp. 386-9.

Forestry Commission (1991), 'Dorset Forests and Heathlands Project', Forestry Commission.

Gardner, J.E. (1989) 'Decision-Making for Sustainable Development', *Environmental Impact Assessment Review* 9, pp. 337-66.

German Government (1990) 'Gesetz zur Umsetzung der Richtlinie des Rates vom 27. Juni 1985 über die Umweltverträglichkeitsprüfung bei bestimmten öffentlichen und privaten Projeckten (85/337/EWG)', *Bundesgesetzblatt* 205, 20 February.

Gibson, J. (1991) 'The integration of pollution control' in *Law, Policy and the Environment*, Basil Blackwell, Oxford, pp. 18-31.

Glasson, J. and Elson, M. (1987) *The Planning and Inquiry Process and Infrastructure Projects*, Major Projects Association, Briefing Paper No. 3.

Glasson, N. (1987) 'Heathland Loss in Nottinghamshire Since 1927', *Landscape Research* 12(1), pp. 13-18.

Goodwin, P. (1991) Chair's Summary in *What Are Roads Worth? Fair Assessment for Transport Expenditure*, presented to a conference organized by Transport 2000 and New Economics Foundation, London.

Gosling, J. (1990) 'The Town and Country (Assessment of Environmental Effects) Regulations 1988: The First Year of Application', Dept. of Land Management and Development, University of Reading.

Government of the Netherlands, Minister of Housing, Physical Planning and Environment (1989a) *National Environmental Policy Plan – To Choose or To Lose*, The Hague, The Netherlands.

Government of the Netherlands, Minister of Housing, Physical Planning and Environment (1989b) 'Environmental Impact Assessment: The

Netherlands – fit for future life', VROM 90512/10-89, The Hague, The Netherlands.

Government of the Netherlands, Minister of Housing, Physical Planning and Environment (1990), *National Environmental Policy Plan Plus*, The Hague, The Netherlands.

Government of the Netherlands, Minister of Housing, Physical Planning and Environment (1991) 'Excerpts from Document on the Effectiveness of the Regulations on Environmental Impact Assessment', The Hague, The Netherlands.

Gow, D.D. (1992) 'Poverty and Natural Resources: Principles for Environmental Management and Sustainable Development', *Environmental Impact Assessment Review* 12 (1/2), pp. 49-65.

Gray, A. and Jenkins, B., eds. (1983) *Policy Analysis and Evaluation in British Government*, Royal Institute of Public Administration, London.

Grimmet, R.F.A and Jones, T.A., eds. (1989) *Important Bird Areas in Europe*, ICBP Technical Publication No. 9, Page Bros, Cambridge.

Grubb, M. et al. (1991) 'Energy Policies and the Greenhouse Effect', *Energy Policy*, 19(10), pp. 911-17.

Gubbay, S. (1990) 'A Future for the Coast: Proposals for a UK Coastal Zone Management Plan', Marine Conservation Society.

Gubbay, S. (1991) 'Management for a crowded coast', *Landscape Design*, 206, pp. 10-12.

Ham, C. and Hill, M. (1984) *The Policy Process in the Modern Capitalist State*, Wheatsheaf Harvester, Brighton.

Hampshire County Council (1984) 'Hampshire's Countryside Heritage, 4: Heathlands', Hampshire County Council.

Hampshire County Council (1989) 'The Future of Hampshire's Heathland', Hampshire Books.

Harrison, P. (1987) *The Greening of Africa*, Paladin Grafton Books, London.

Hatton, C. (1992) World Wide Fund for Nature, personal communication, 21 January.

Heap, J. (1992) English Nature, personal communication, 20 February.

Helm, D. (1991) 'Privatization and Environmental Regulation in the Water and Electricity Industries', *Royal Bank of Scotland Review* 172, pp. 30-7.

Henkel, M. (1991) *Government, Evaluation and Change*, Jessica Knightley, London.

Her Majesty's Government (1985) *Lifting the Burden*, Cmnd 9571, HMSO, London.

Her Majesty's Government (1991) Government *Observations on the 13th Report from the House of Lords Select Committee on the European Communities on Energy and the Environment*, HMG, London.

Her Majesty's Treasury (1988) *Policy Evaluation: A Guide for Managers*, HMSO, London.

Her Majesty's Treasury (1991) *Economic Appraisal in Central Government*, HMSO, London.

Herson, A.I. and K.M. Bogdan (1991) 'Cumulative Impact Analysis under NEPA', *The Environmental Professional* 13, pp. 100-6.

HMSO (1971) *International Convention on Wetlands of International Importance, Especially as Waterfowl Habitat, (Ramsar)*, Cmnd 6465, HMSO, London.

Hogwood, B. (1987) *From Crisis to Complacency? Shaping Public Policy in Britain*, Oxford University Press, Oxford.

Houghton J.T., Jenkins, G.J. and Ephraums, J.J., eds. (1990) *Climate Change: The IPCC Scientific Assessment*, Cambridge University Press, Cambridge.

House of Commons Energy Committee (1989) *Energy Policy Implications of the Greenhouse Effect*, HMSO, London.

House of Commons Energy Committee (1992) *Consequences of Electricity Privatisation*, Second Report 1991-1992 113-I, HMSO, London.

House of Commons Environment Committee (1986) *Planning: Appeals, Call In and Major Public Inquiries*, Session 1985-86 Fifth Report, HMSO, London.

House of Commons Environment Committee (1992) *Coastal Zone Protection and Planning*, HMSO, London.

House of Commons Parliamentary Debates (1991), *Weekly Hansard* 190(1557), 7 - 10 May, HMSO, London.

House of Lords Select Committee on the European Committees (1991) *Energy and the Environment*, 13th Report 1990-1991 (HL Paper 62), HMSO, London.

Houston, J. (1991) 'The Sefton Coast Management Scheme', *Landscape Design* 206, p. 31.

Howarth, W. (1991) 'Crimes against the Aquatic Environment', in Churchill, R. et al., *Law, Policy and the Environment*, Basil Blackwell, Oxford, pp. 95-107.

Huisman, H. (1990) 'Application of EIA to Policies and Programs: The Case of Provincial Waste Management Plans', European Summer School on Environmental Decision-Making on Waste Management, 26 June, Vrije Universiteit, Brussels.

International Energy Agency (1989) *Energy and the Environment: Policy Overview*, OECD/IEA, Paris.

International Energy Agency (1992) *Global Energy: the Changing Outlook*, OECD/IEA, Paris.

Jacobs, M. (1991) *The Green Economy*, Pluto Press, London.

Joint Unit for Research on the Urban Environment, University of Aston (1977) 'Assessing the Environmental Impact of Transport Plans and Policies', memorandum to the Environment and Consumer Protection Service.

Jones, C.T (1991) 'Managing the European Coast', *Landscape Design*, December 1991/January 1992.

Jones, T. (1992) *Environmental Impact Assessment for Coal*, IEACR/46, IEA Coal Research, London.

Keay, M. (1991) *Gas Regulation, the Environment and Energy Efficiency*, OFGAS, London.

Ketcham, D.E. (1992) US Forest Service, personal communication, 16 July.

Keymer, R. (1992) English Nature, personal communication, 5 February.

Kleinschmidt, V. (1991) 'Strategic Environmental Assessment of Technological Research Proposals', *EIA Review* 6, p.4.

Leach, G. (1991) 'Policies to Reduce Energy Use and Carbon Emissions in the UK', *Energy Policy* 19(10), pp. 918-25.

Lee, N. and Colley, R. (1990) *Reviewing Environmental Statements*, Occasional Paper No. 24, EIA Centre, University of Manchester, Manchester.

Lee, N. and Wood, C.M. (1984) 'Environmental impact assessment procedures within the European Economic Community', in Roberts, R.D. and Roberts, T.M., eds., *Planning and Ecology*, Chapman and Hall, London, pp. 128-34.

Lenstra, W.J. (1991) 'The Role of the Netherlands National Environmental Policy Plan (NEPP) in Energy Policy', in Barker, T., ed., *The Future for Economic Growth: Britain in 2010*, Cambridge Econometrics, Cambridge.

Leopold, L.B., Clark, F.E., Hanshaw, B.B. and Balsley, J.R. (1971) *A procedure for evaluating environmental impact*, US Geological Survey Circular 645, Department of Interior, Washington, DC.

Lewis, D. (1992) 'Orimulsion's Tarnished Promise', *Geographical Magazine* LXIV(7), pp. 16-9.

Linklaters and Paines (1990) 'The White Paper on the Environment: A Summary of the Government's recent proposals', Linklaters and Paines, London.

Lowe, P. and Flynn, A. (1989) 'Environmental politics and policy in the 1980s', in Mohan, J., ed., *The Political Geography of Contemporary Britain*, Macmillan, London.

Manning, M. (1991) *The Role of Environmental Assessments in Power System Planning*, paper presented to conference on Advances in Environmental Assessment, London.

Marshall, T. (1992) 'How Green is Your Region?', *Town and Country Planning* 61(1), pp. 22-25.

Martin, I. (1990) 'Energy Planning Locally: The Cornwall Experience', *Proceedings of the TCPA Conference on Planning for Sustainable Development*, TCPA, London.

McCormick, J. (1991) *British Politics and the Environment*, Earthscan, London.

McGowan, F. (1990) 'The Development of Orimulsion and Venezuelan Oil Strategy', *Energy Policy* 18(10), pp. 913-26.

Meadows, D.H., Meadows, D.L., Randers, J. and Behrens, W.W.III (1972) *Limits to Growth*, Earth Island, London.

Merrill, F. (1981) 'Areawide Environmental Impact Assessment Guidebook', *Environmental Impact Assessment Review* 2, pp. 204-7.

MAFF (1991a) *John Gummer holds flood and coastal defence policy: Environmental Review*, MAFF Press Release 433/91.

MAFF (1991b) *Periodic Review of Flood and Coastal Defence Policy: Background Paper*, MAFF Flood Defence Division.

Montgomery, T. (1990) 'An Introduction to the Concept of Tiered Environmental Assessment', paper presented at workshop on Assessing Environmental Assessments: Quality and Content, 20 Sept., Bristol.

Murphy, T. (1992) European Bank for Reconstruction and Development, personal communication, 14 July.

Nature Conservancy Council (1981) 'The Conservation of Lowland Heathland', Nature Conservancy Council, Peterborough.

Nature Conservancy Council (1987a) 'Lundy – Britain's first Marine Nature Reserve', *Topical Issues* 3(1), Nature Conservancy Council, Peterborough, pp.1-2.

Nature Conservancy Council (1987b) *Birds, Bogs and Forestry: The Peatlands of Caithness and Sutherland*, Nature Conservancy Council, Peterborough.

Nature Conservancy Council (1988) *Heathland Habitat Network News* 1(1), Nature Conservancy Council, Peterborough.

Nature Conservancy Council (1990) 'Handbook for Phase I Habitat Survey – A Technique for Environmental Audit', Nature Conservancy Council, Peterborough.

Nature Conservancy Council (1991) *Nature Conservation and Estuaries in Great Britain*, Nature Conservancy Council, Peterborough.

Nature Conservancy Council/Nottinghamshire County Council (undated) 'A Heathland Strategy for Nottinghamshire', NCC.

Nature Conservancy Council/Surrey County Council (1988) 'A Strategy for Surrey Heathland', Surrey County Council Commercial Services.

Nature Conservancy Council West Midlands/Staffordshire County Council (1985) 'A Survey of the Lowland Heathlands of Staffordshire and the West Midlands County', NCC/SCC.

Nature Conservancy Council/Staffordshire County Council (1989) 'Survey of the Lowland Heathland in Staffordshire and the West Midlands County'.

New Forest District Council (1988) 'Report of the New Forest Review Group', New Forest District Council.

Newson, M. (1992) 'Land and water convergence, divergence and progress in UK policy', *Land Use Policy*, 9(2).

Nijkamp, P. and Volwahsen, A. (1990) 'New Directions in Integrated Regional Energy Planning', *Energy Policy* 18(8), pp. 764-73.

Norfolk County Council (1990) 'Norfolk Structure Plan Review', Norfolk County Council.

North West Water (1988) *Fylde Coastal Waters Improvements*, North West Water, Preston.

NORWEB/ETSU (1989) 'Prospects for Renewable Energy in the NORWEB Area', NORWEB/ETSU.

Nuffield Foundation Committee of Inquiry (1986) *Town and Country Planning*, Nuffield Foundation, London.

Office of Electricity Regulation (1991) *Energy Efficiency: Consultation Paper*, Birmingham.

O'Riordan, T. and Hey, R., eds. (1976) *Environmental Impact Assessment*, Saxon House, Farnborough.

O'Riordan, T. and Sewell, W.R.D. (1981) *Project Appraisal and Policy Review*, John Wiley & Sons, Ltd., Chichester.

O'Riordan, T., Kemp, R. and Purdue, M. (1988) *Sizewell B: An Anatomy of the Inquiry*, Macmillan, London.

OECD (1988) *Environmental Impacts of Renewable Energy: The OECD Compass Project*, OECD, Paris.

OECD (1991) *The State of the Environment*, OECD, Paris.

Orloff, N. (1980) *The National Environmental Policy Act: Cases and Materials*, Bureau of National Affairs, Washington, DC.

Outer Circle Policy Unit (1979) *The Big Public Inquiry*, OCPU, London.

Owens, S. (1990) 'Energy', in Bayliss Smith, T. and Owens, S., eds., *Britain's Changing Environment from the Air*, Cambridge University Press, Cambridge.

Owens, S. (1991) *Energy-Conscious Planning – A Case for Action*, CPRE, London.

Owens, S. and Owens, P.L. (1991) *Environment, Resources and Conservation*, Cambridge University Press, Cambridge.

Parker, S., Cocklin, C. and Hay, J. (1990) *Cumulative Environmental Change*, Environmental Science Occasional Publications CEC 01-03, University of Auckland, Auckland.

Patrick, C. (1988) 'Environmental Assessment of Policy Proposals', in *Environmental Impact Assessment and Management, 11th International Seminar*, CEMP, University of Aberdeen.

Pearce, D. (1989) 'Sustainable Development and Environmental Impact Appraisal', Keynote address to 10th International Seminar on Environmental Impact Assessment and Management, University of Aberdeen, July 1989.

Pearce, D., Markandya, A. and Barbier, E. (1989) *Blueprint for a Green Economy*, Earthscan, London.

Pearce, F. (1992) 'Last Chance to Save the Planet?', *New Scientist*, 134(1823), pp 24-8.

Pickles, S. (1992) 'Discuss the feasibility of preparing a strategic environmental assessment...', essay written as part of MSc course in Planning at Oxford Polytechnic.

Pollitt, C. and Harrison, S. (1992) *Handbook of Public Service Management*, Blackwell Business, Oxford.

Purves, G. (1992) Scottish Office, personal communication, 20 March.

Ratick, S. and Lakshamanan, T.R. (1983) 'An Overview of the Strategic Environmental Assessment System', *System and Models for Energy and Environmental Analysis*, Gower, Aldershot.

Reddish, A. and Rand, M. (1991) 'The Environmental Effects of Present

Energy Policies', in Blunden, J. and Reddish, A., eds., *Energy, Resources and Environment*, Open University/Hodder and Stoughton, London.

Rees, W.E. (1988) 'A Role for Environmental Assessment in Achieving Sustainable Development', *Environmental Impact Assessment Review* 8, pp. 273-91.

Review (1992) 'Review Update: Studies on UK Potential for Renewable Energy', Vol. 18, p. 19.

Roberts, R.D. and Roberts, T.M. (1984) *Planning and Ecology*, Chapman and Hall, London.

Rothwell, P.I. and Housden, S.D. (1990) *Turning the Tide: a future for estuaries*, RSPB, Sandy, Beds.

Rowell, T.A. (1991) 'SSSIs: A Health Check: A Review of the Statutory Protection Afforded to SSSIs in Great Britain', Wildlife Link, London.

Royal Commission on Environmental Pollution (1976) *Nuclear Power and the Environment* Report 6, Cmnd 6618, HMSO, London.

Royal Society for the Protection of Birds (1988) *The Reform of the Common Agricultural Policy: New Opportunities for Wildlife and the Environment. A Discussion Paper*, RSPB, Sandy, Beds.

Royal Society for the Protection of Birds (1991a) *Coastal Zone Planning: Evidence to the House of Commons Select Committee on the Environment*, RSPB, Sandy, Beds.

Royal Society for the Protection of Birds (1991b) *Evidence Submitted to the House of Commons Select Committee on Energy into Renewable Energy*, RSPB, Sandy, Beds.

Royal Society for the Protection of Birds (undated) *Response by RSPB to SOEND. Consultation on Guidance on the Location of Marine Fish Farms*, RSPB, Edinburgh.

Sandford, R. (1992) 'Conflict Management, Dispute Resolution, and Ecologically Sustainable Development', *Environmental Impact Assessment Review* 12, pp. 181-3.

Schrage, W. (1991) 'UNECE EIA Activities during 1991', *EIA Newsletter* 6, pp. 14-15.

Scottish Office (1991) *Guidance on the Location of Marine Fish Farms, Consultative Draft*, Environment Department, December.

Scottish Wildlife and Countryside Link (1988) *Marine Fish Farming in Scotland: A Discussion Paper*, SWCL, Perth.

Scottish Wildlife and Countryside Link (1990) *Marine Salmon Farming in Scotland: A Review*, SWCL, Perth.

Secretary of State for the Environment et al. (1990) *This Common Inheritance: Britain's Environmental Strategy*, Cmnd 1200, HMSO, London.

Secretary of State for the Environment et al. (1991) *This Common Inheritance: First Year Report*, Cm 1655, HMSO, London.

Sidaway, R. (1991) *A Review of Marina Developments in Southern England*, RSPB/WWF Joint Report, August.

Sigal, L. and Cada, G. (1991) 'NEPA Compliance Auditing', *The Environmental Professional* 13, pp. 174-7.

Sigal, L. and Webb, J.W. (1989) 'The Programmatic Environmental Impact Statement: Its Purpose and Use', *The Environmental Professional* 11, pp. 14-24.

Slater, D. (1992) 'Integrated Pollution Control – The Role of Environmental Assessments and Environmental Management Systems', paper presented at First Membership Conference, Institute of Environmental Assessment, Birmingham, 6 July.

Smith, B. (1976) *Policy-Making in British Government: An Analysis of Power and Rationality*, Martin Robertson, London.

Smith, H.D and Lalawani, C.S. (1992) 'The North Sea: Development and Conservation', *Scottish Geographical Magazine* 107, (3), pp.179-86

Staffordshire County Council and Countryside Commission (undated) 'Heaths in Staffordshire', Staffordshire County Council.

Staffordshire Wildlife Trust, Royal Society for the Protection of Birds, and Royal Society for Nature Conservation (1991) 'Action for Staffordshire Heathland'.

Standing Advisory Committee on Trunk Road Assessment (1992) *Assessing the Environmental Impact of Road Schemes*, HMSO, London.

State of California (1986) *The California Environmental Quality Act*, Office of Planning and Research, Sacramento, CA.

Stedman, B.J and Hill, T. (1992) 'Introduction to the Special Issue: Perspectives on Sustainable Development', *Environmental Impact Assessment Review* 12(1/2), pp. 1-10.

Stern, R.M. (1990) 'Environment and Health Data in Europe as a Tool for Risk Management: Needs, Uses, and Strategies', Paper presented at International Seminar on Environmental Impact Assessment and Management, 8-21 July, University of Aberdeen.

Stoney, P. (1989) 'The Mersey Barrage: Panacea or Hot Air', *Merseyside Economic and Business Prospect* 4, p.2.

Street, E. (1992) Kent County Council, personal communication.

Strong, M. (1992) 'Energy, Environment and Development', *Energy Policy* 20(6), pp. 490-5.

Teesside Power Ltd. (1990) *Teesside Pipelines Project Environmental Statement*, Trident Consultants, London.

Thames Water Authority (1988) *Lower Colne Flood Defence Scheme*, Thames Water Authority.

Therivel, R. (1991) *Directory of Environmental Statements 1988-1991*, School of Planning, Oxford Polytechnic, Oxford.

Therivel, R., Wilson, E., Thompson, S. and Heaney, D. (1992) *Environmental Impact Assessment: Application at the Strategic Level*, report for the RSPB.

Tomlinson, P. (1986) 'Environmental assessment in the UK: Implementation of the EEC Directive', *Town Planning Review* 57(4), pp. 458-86.

Tomlinson, P. (1989) 'Environmental Statements: Guidance for Review and Audit', *The Planner*, 75(28), pp. 12-15.

Town and Country Planning Association (1992) *Draft Summary Report of the Working Group on Sustainable Development*, unpublished.

Treweek, J. (1992) Institute of Terrestrial Ecology, personal communication, 6 January.

Tubbs, C. (1985) 'The Decline and Present Status of the English Lowland Heaths and Their Vertebrates', *Focus on Nature Conservation*, NCC.

Tucker, J.J. (1982) 'Heathland Interest Register: An Initial Register of People with Management and/or Research Interests in all Types of Heath, Dune-Heath and Moor'. Privately published, Kidderminster.

Turner, R.K. (1988) *Sustainable Environmental Management*, Belhaven Press, London.

United Nations Economic Commission for Europe (1991a) *Policies and Systems of Environmental Impact Assessment*, ECE/ENVWA/15, United Nations, New York.

United Nations Economic Commission for Europe (1991b) 'Convention on Environmental Impact Assessment in a Transboundary Context', (E/ECE/1250), 24 February.

United Nations Environment Programme (1989) *Environmental Data Report 1989/90*, Blackwell Reference, Oxford.

Urwin, J. (1988) *Aussie Rules Planning*, Birmingham City Council Development Department, Birmingham.

US Council on Environmental Quality (1978) *Regulations for Implementing the Procedural Provisions of the National Environmental Policy Act*, 40 CFR 1500-1508.

US Department of Energy (1989) *Clean Coal Technology Demonstration Program Final Programmatic Environmental Impact Statement*, DOE/EIS-0146, Washington, DC.

US Department of Energy (1992a) *National Environmental Policy Act; Implementing Procedures and Guidelines Revocation; Final Rule and Notice*, 10 CFR 1021, 24 April.

US Department of Energy (1992b) *Implementation Plan: Nuclear Weapons Complex Reconfiguration Programmatic Environmental Impact Statement*, Washington, DC.

US Department of Energy (1992c) *Draft Implementation Plan for the Programmatic Environmental Impact Statement for the Department of Energy Environmental Restoration and Waste Management Program*, Washington, DC.

US Department of Housing and Urban Development (1981) *Areawide Environmental Assessment*, Office of Policy Development and Research, HUD.

US Department of the Interior (1980) *Departmental Manual*, Part 516: National Environmental Policy Act of 1969, 3/18/80 #2244.

US Department of Transportation (1991) *Final Programmatic Environmental Impact Statement for the Terminal Doppler Weather Radar Site Determination*

Program, Federal Aviation Administration, Office of Surveillance, Washington, DC.

US Government (1970) *National Environmental Policy Act of 1969*, as amended, 42 USC 4321-4347, 1 Jan.

UVP Report 3/91 contains a number of articles on SEA in Germany.

van der Lee, R. (1992) Dutch Ministry of Housing, Physical Planning and Environment, personal communication, 4 and 18 February.

Wagner, D. (1991a) 'UVP für Politiken, Programme und Planungen in den USA', to be published in *UVP Report*, 1992.

Wagner, J. (1991b) 'Überlegungen zur Einführung einer Umweltverträglichkeitsprüfung für Programme und Pläne in das Deutsche Recht', *UVP Report* 3(91), pp. 98-9.

Wagner, D. (1991c) Verein zur Förderung der Umweltvertraglichkeitsprüfung, personal communication, 18 October.

Wandesforde-Smith, G. (1980) 'Environmental Impact Assessment and the Politics of Development in Europe', Chapter 8 in T. O'Riordan and R.K. Turner, eds., *Progress in Resource Management and Environmental Planning, Vol. 2*, John Wiley and Sons, Chichester, pp. 205-37.

Warren, A. (1990) 'The Scope for Conservation', *Proceedings of the TCPA Conference on Planning for Sustainable Development*, TCPA, London.

Wathern, P., ed. (1988) *Environmental Impact Assessment*, Unwin Hyman, London.

Wathern, P., Young, S.N., Brown, I.W. and Roberts, D.A. (1987) 'Assessing the Impacts of Policy: A Framework and an Application', *Landscape and Urban Planning* 14, pp. 321-30.

Wathern, P., Brown, I., Roberts, D. and Young, S. (1988) 'Assessing the Environmental Impacts of Policy', Chapter 6 in Clark, M. and Herington, J., eds., *The Role of Environmental Impact Assessment in the Planning Process*, Mansell, London.

Watt Committee on Energy (M.A. Loughten, ed.) (1990a) *Renewable Energy Sources*, Report No. 22, Elsevier Applied Science, Barking, Essex.

Watt Committee on Energy (Thurlow, G., ed.) (1990b) *Technological Responses to the Greenhouse Effect*, Report No. 23, Elsevier Applied Science, Barking, Essex.

Webb, A. (1991) *The Future for UK Environment Policy*, Economist Intelligence Unit, London.

Webb, N. (1986) *Heathlands – A Natural History of Britain's Lowland Heaths*, The New Naturalist, Collins, London.

Webber, S. (1992) Sefton Borough Council, personal communication, 30 January.

Wells, C. (1991) 'Impact Assessment in New Zealand: The Resource Management Act', *EIA Newsletter* 6, pp. 19-20.

West Midlands Regional Forum of Local Authorities (1991) *The West Midlands: Your Region, Your Future*, West Midlands Regional Forum.

Westman, W.E. (1985) *Ecology, Impact Assessment and Environmental Planning*, John Wiley, New York.

Wildlife Link (undated), *A selection of case studies illustrating the need for coastal zone management in the UK*, Wildlife Link.

Winpenny, J.T. (1991) *Values for the Environment*, HMSO, London.

Wishart, C. (1992) Highland Regional Council, personal communication, 18 March.

Wood, C. (1981) 'The Impact of the European Commission's Directive on Environmental Planning in the United Kingdom', *Planning Outlook* 24(3), pp. 92-8.

Wood, C. (1988) 'EIA in Plan Making', Chapter 6 in P. Wathern, ed. *Environmental Impact Assessment*, Unwin Hyman, London.

Wood, C. (1991) 'EIA of Policies, Plans and Programmes', *EIA Newsletter* 5, pp. 2-3.

Wood, C. and Djeddour, M. (1991) 'Strategic Environmental Assessment: EA of Policies, Plans and Programmes', submitted to the Bulletin of the International Association for Impact Assessment, University of Manchester.

Woodliffe, J. (1991) 'Environmental Awareness and UK Energy Policy', in Churchill, R. et al., *Law, Policy and the Environment*, Basil Blackwell, Oxford.

World Bank (1991) *Environmental Assessment Sourcebook Vol. 1: Policies, Procedures and Cross-Sectoral Issues*, Technical Paper 139, World Bank, Washington, DC.

World Commission on Environment and Development (Brundtland Commission) (1987) *Our Common Future*, Oxford University Press, Oxford.

The RSPB

The Royal Society for the Protection of Birds is Europe's largest wildlife conservation organization, with nearly a million members. This huge and growing membership supports the Society because it has positive ideas, a vision for the future and a record of achievement.

Too often, environmentalists are accused of idealism – the RSPB's approach is, however, practical, realistic and informed. It exists to safeguard our natural heritage of wild birds and their habitats. The RSPB:

* researches conservation issues, and proposes and implements solutions to the problems;

* develops programmes of action to safeguard our rarest species;

* campaigns for UK government and EC policy changes sympathetic to wildlife;

* works with a network of conservation organisations in all the EC member states and beyond;

* buys special areas of land in the UK to manage as nature reserves for the benefit of wildlife and people – currently 120 sites throughout the country, covering 76,700 ha;

* acts to promote the conservation of migratory birds and threatened species worldwide;

* places a strong emphasis on youth and education;

* works with landowners, industry and the public to provide a better future for wildlife.

RSPB Headquarters, The Lodge, Sandy, Bedfordshire SG19 2DL.
Tel: 0767 680551   Fax: 0767 692365
RSPB Scottish Headquarters, 17 Regent Terrace, Edinburgh EH7 5BN
Tel: 031 557 3136   Fax: 031 557 6275
RSPB Wales Office, Bryn Aderyn, The Bank, Newtown, Powys SY16 2AB
Tel: 0686 626678   Fax: 0686 626794
RSPB Northern Ireland Office, Belvoir Park Forest, Belfast BT8 4QT
Tel: 0232 491547   Fax: 0232 491669

Index